FROM FAITH TO DOUBT...AND LIFE AS A FAILED BELIEVER

Phil,
Sorry I didn't warn you that this was coming!

William

Copyright © 2011 Wallace Murphree

ISBN 978-1-60910-652-2

All rights reserved. No part of this publication may be reproduced, stored in a retrieval system, or transmitted in any form or by any means, electronic, mechanical, recording or otherwise, without the prior written permission of the author.

Published in the United States by Booklocker.com, Inc., Bangor, Maine.

Printed in the United States of America on acid-free paper.

Booklocker.com, Inc.
2011

First Edition

FROM FAITH TO DOUBT...AND LIFE AS A FAILED BELIEVER

Wallace Murphree

Preface

During my years of teaching philosophy I tried to be even-handed in my treatment of atheism and theism, and I think my own agnosticism served me well for this purpose. However, in addition to being able to present and argue both views in class I always felt I had further contributions—insights from my own experiences—that might be of value to those personally struggling with this issue, but I had no institutional opportunity to share them there.

This memoir is my attempt to share these insights now. It is offered in hope that the record of my own struggle and a sketch of my skeptical point of view that ensued can be of assistance to others who are undergoing a crisis of faith. Moreover, it is also offered in hope of helping staunch believers appreciate the predicament of those facing the onset of religious uncertainty.

I have wanted to write such a book for a long time, but probably would never have begun it on my own. Accordingly, I acknowledge a great indebtedness to my brother-in-law, Ken Corson, whose encouragement to write in my retirement has been persistent.

Contents

Prologue 1

Chapter 1: Childhood 5

Chapter 2: Youth 10

Chapter 3: Facing the Question 27

Chapter 4: Philosophical Arguments 34

The Teleological Argument 34

The Cosmological Argument 36

The Ontological Argument 38

The Moral Argument 41

The Problem of Evil 44

Criticism 48

Chapter 5: Looking Back 52

Chapter 6: Is Christianity Evil? A Question of Honesty 63

Belief-premium Christianity 68

(1) Self-interest 68

Self-interest and Dishonesty 74

(2) Duty 76

Duty and Dishonesty 78

Summary: Belief-premium Christianity 80

Love-premium Christianity 82

Chapter 7: Hurting Those Who Cared 86

Wallace Murphree

Chapter 8: Living in Doubt... **94**

    Reality 95

    Ethics.. 100

    Faith 106

    Death.. 109

Epilogue **117**

Prologue

In introductory classes in philosophy it is not uncommon for instructors to assign short, argumentative papers in the attempt to lead students to do "original philosophy"—that is, to get them to philosophize themselves, rather than merely to read what other philosophers have written.

For such exercises a list of popular philosophical issues is usually provided, such as,

> Do human beings have free will?
> Are ethical laws absolute?
> Does there exist a God?
> Etc.,

from which students are to select a topic. The assignment then is (1) to adopt a position on the selected issue, and (2) to construct a rational defense for that position, i.e., to provide a rational justification—a logical argument—to show why that position is the one that ought to be believed.

Contrary to popular anecdotes about philosophy classes, *which* side is taken is of no concern to the instructor (at least, it should not be); rather the features assessed when the instructor reads the papers simply are:

> Does this paper demonstrate an understanding of what the issue is?

and

> Does the defense of the side taken show original thought on the part of the student?

Indeed, it is not required that the defense be especially good; rather, it is only required that it be attempted, and that the student make as strong a case as he or she can for it.

However, providing a compelling defense for any philosophical position is an extremely difficult matter, and after doing their very best good students usually realize that their attempt was unsuccessful. So in addition to getting them personally involved in the subject matter, discovering the difficulty of creating successful defenses also helps them appreciate the classical arguments for and against the various positions when they are studied in the class later on.

But, of course, sometimes student responses miss the point altogether. I specifically remember one neat, carefully typed paper on good stationery (before word processors) that was entitled "Why I Believe God Exists." It went something like this:

> My grandfather was a preacher, my father is a deacon, and my mother teaches Sunday school, and at a very early age they taught me that God exists. Moreover, my aunts and uncles have prayed all my life that I would grow up to be a strong Christian, and all my close friends are regular churchgoers. In addition, the president of my country and the governor of my state believe in God, and the Pledge of Allegiance attests to His reality....
>
> Etc. Etc.
>
> And these are the reasons why I believe God exists.

But this paper was not acceptable. Of course, the claims it contained were no doubt true and they showed a degree of self-awareness on the part of the student. But the paper contained no attempt to *justify* the belief it reported; instead, it simply contained the student's description of what *caused* her to start out with this belief rather than an alternative one.

From Faith to Doubt...and Life as a Failed Believer

I suppose I responded something like: "Fine, this reports how you were reared in this view; but other people are reared in other views. So, what reason do you have for supposing the view you were reared in is the correct one? What rational justification can you give for still believing it now that you are able to think about it?"

Of course, the question as to what, exactly, constitutes a rationally justified belief is itself a matter of live philosophical debate, and most, if not all, would agree that small children are not irrational for accepting what they are taught by nurturing adults. But on the other hand, most, if not all, would also agree that as children mature, it would not be rational for them to continue accepting beliefs on the *sole* basis that they were so taught by nurturing adults when they were children.

Chapter 1 Childhood

Like the student, I was taught to believe by my parents. My grandfather and father were Methodist ministers, as were two of my father's four brothers; and from the beginning my life was steeped in a religious outlook on things. Life on earth was depicted as a test to determine where one's eternal afterlife would be spent, and so it was the highest duty of parents to rear the children in the "straight and narrow way" to life everlasting.

My earliest memories are from our daily, family devotions in which we would sing, and read or quote scripture, and pray. Often my father would quote the first verse from a chapter in the Bible for a night or two and then he would move on to the second verse, and my mother would quote the first. And then, as they moved up another verse my sister, Sarah, would be assigned the first and then my older brother, (Jon) Tal; so, ordinarily I would already know each new verse by the time it became my responsibility to quote it. By this method I'm sure I had several full chapters of the Bible memorized before I started to school.

We lived on a small, wooded farm outside of Wedowee (we-DOW-ee), Alabama. My father had been appointed pastor of the northern Methodist church in Wedowee shortly after he and Mother married. Then, when the northern and southern churches unified, Daddy "localized" and the pastor of the southern church became pastor of the combined congregation. Dad, in turn, was appointed to smaller, rural churches in the county and began teaching English (and later Latin) in high school as our family's primary source of income.

There were five of us children. I was the middle, and my younger two brothers were born after Dad began teaching. When they got old enough to be left with a sitter, Mother started teaching, too.

We children and Mother usually attended Sunday morning and evening worship services at our home church in Wedowee and often Wednesday night prayer meeting as well. In summers, we worked on the farm during the day but would attend the evening sessions during the church's revival meeting week, as well as those of the neighboring country churches where my father pastored.

Our big event each summer was Camp Meeting. After the crops were laid by we would pack our clothes for the ten-day stay in a cabin on Brasher's Springs camp ground some eighty miles away, where my grandfather (and later my father) was vice president. Here three main services and a special youth service were held daily, and prayer meetings and Bible study sessions often emerged between times. There would always be spirited and joyful music, and the evangelists would bring powerful messages that would conclude with moving invitations for sinners to repent and the saved to become sanctified.

During these early years I had no reason to doubt this religious interpretation of everything. Indeed, it didn't occur to me that it might be an "interpretation" at all (in the sense that alternative interpretations might be advanced); instead, the details of this world picture were simply taken as facts, and the existence of God was as unchallenged as the existence of gravity.

Furthermore, like gravity, the alleged religious facts seemed to be borne out in my experience. For example, from an early age I would feel Satan tempting me to disobey my parents, and I could sense the Holy Spirit urging me to do what was right. Also, I would feel God's presence in church, at Camp Meeting, in family devotions, and often alone on the farm; and these emotions were nearly as easily identifiable as anger, love, or fear.

Moreover, so far as I knew, every acquaintance of my youth held essentially this same view; at least they all believed that the God of Christianity exists. Of course, there were plenty of "sinners" around. But they all believed in God and intended to give up the life of sin

From Faith to Doubt...and Life as a Failed Believer

and get forgiveness before they died, for otherwise they believed they would be eternally "lost," and go to hell. (The first professing atheist I remember meeting was when I was in the army.)

I'm not sure, but I think I may have had a passing doubt about the existence of God when I learned that Santa Claus was not real. It seems I remember wondering how old children would be when the adults confessed that the God-story is also a fairy tale. But it was a year or two later, when I was in the third grade, that I had my first really disturbing doubt. The class had read a piece in the *Weekly Reader* about Eskimos which included a vivid description of day-to-day life of a boy our own age. It provided accounts of dress, diet, chores, living conditions, family relationships, and a little about the religious beliefs and practices of his community. The teacher asked us to imagine ourselves being born and living there. I enjoyed the exercise, and could nearly pretend myself to be the Eskimo boy—except for the religion, because I "knew" it was wrong. However, I tried very hard, for two or three days at least, to see everything from his point of view. It was difficult for me to hold onto my ideas, and I would lose track and have to repeat my thoughts again and again. For starters each time, I would suppose the Eskimo boy received a *Weekly Reader* telling about a boy in Alabama (me), our ways, and our religion; then I took turns imaging myself to be that Eskimo boy, and then letting myself be me.

As myself, I *knew* the Eskimo boy accepted a false religion, but I realized that he accepted it because his parents taught him it was true and all his friends and acquaintances agreed with it. Then, as the Eskimo boy, I *thought I knew* the Alabama boy accepted a false religion, but that he likewise accepted it because that was what his parents taught him and it was what all his friends and acquaintances believed. But this was as close as I could bring the two positions to compare—: I *knew* his religion was wrong, but he just *thought he knew* that my religion was wrong.

I realized that if I had been born to his parents, I would believe as he did, and that if he had been born to my parents, he would believe as I did. Still I just couldn't allow credence to the possibility that his view might actually be correct and mine false, although I came so close that it frightened me—which I thought must be a warning from the Holy Spirit.

The one point of difference I arrived at that finally allowed me some peace was that my parents were better educated than his; so, I concluded, if Christianity had been false, my school-teaching parents would surely have discovered it already. Deep down I may have known this answer would not do in the long run, but it did allow me to turn loose of the matter at the time.

Although our religion held that belief was a prerequisite for salvation, I was not concerned about losing mine once I had turned loose of the Eskimo boy exercise. Rather, I just assumed that the more I learned and understood, the more obvious the truth of the teachings would become.

However, I did worry about going to hell when I died; but I felt my greatest danger came from the possibility that I might be temporarily lured into sinful pleasure and then, like a "dope fiend," become spiritually blinded until I would have passed the point of no return. Of course, I promised myself again and again never to venture into such sin, but I knew that even the sincerest vows might yield to temptation if they were simply made and forgotten. So in an attempt to keep my vows from becoming casual and weak, I would often quote a haunting poem to myself about a boy whose promises failed, and whose life became "wrecked by the wine cup." The final lines were:

> After the days of childhood
> After a mother's prayer
> After the years of manhood
> Freighted with joys and care
> After a thousand chances

From Faith to Doubt...and Life as a Failed Believer

After the final call
Bitter the wail of the spirit:
Lost after all![1]

---

[1] Charlie D. Tillman, *Select Revival Songs,* ed. Rev. E.B. Farrar (Dalton GA: The A.J. Showalter Co., Dalton GA, 1897), 101. [Instructions read: Can be sung to the tune "After the Ball."]

Chapter 2 Youth

Because of their roles in school and church, my parents were in the public eye more than most; they were friendly, generous and, so far as I knew, they were highly respected by everyone even though some thought their views to be extreme. In a way they were very social, for the door to our home was always open and there seemed to be no end to the old friends and students, or people with problems seeking their counsel, who would drop by. Moreover, they freely allowed us children to have friends over, and for us to spend the night with our friends in turn. So, in a way my family was fully involved "in the world"; however, my parents believed that Christians were not to be "of the world," but set apart from it instead.

The reason Christians were to be set apart was that the world was evil, and worldliness was a sin. Of course, God was not responsible for the evil since the world he created was perfect. That is, the original Garden of Eden had no weeds in it, so to speak; and the lamb and lion lived in peace there. But with the sin of Adam and Eve, the world "fell" and became depraved; and with The Fall the garden had to be cultivated by the sweat of the brow, and the animal kingdom became a system of predators and prey.

This view provided the general backdrop to my parents' understanding of the place of humankind in the scheme of things. It was never argued, although Biblical references to its truth were often cited and illustrative instances of it were often pointed out. For example, I remember once when we were trying to rescue our vegetable garden from the weeds, Dad called Tal's and my attention to a big, green worm on a tomato plant in his row. The worm seemed to be eating *our* tomato plant as fast as it could, while its back was covered with wasp larvae that were feeding on it. Tal and I watched the miserable scene a few seconds before Dad plucked the leaf and

From Faith to Doubt...and Life as a Failed Believer

trampled it, worm, and larvae into the soil, and said, "This is not the way God created things."

Furthermore, Dad believed that human nature was also a victim of The Fall. That is, he believed that little children *naturally* deceive, steal, bully, etc., and that human appetites are *naturally* unattuned to the needs of the body; likewise, he thought that many things that *naturally* attract us psychologically are ultimately destructive of the soul.

But he didn't believe the ruination to be total. Rather, as with a work of art that had been exposed to the elements, he believed one could still glimpse the original, overall grandeur of nature even though the deterioration of the details were painfully obvious. And he didn't see human nature as being irremediably sinful; indeed, he saw the beauty of saintliness in those who were fully surrendered to Christ.

So, while my parents were fully involved in the sinful world, they understood the role of a Christian to be that of trying to lead others out of it, and urging them to forego the momentary and self-destructive pleasures it had to offer. And while they believed they could make a difference, they also accepted the view that most people, nevertheless, would not be saved and would suffer eternal damnation.

The religious call to be set apart kept us children from participating in many of secular activities that the families of our classmates found quite acceptable. For example, among other things, my siblings and I were not allowed to attend movies, play football (or attend the games), swim in public pools, read comics books, play cards, dance, drink Coca Colas (or any caffeinated beverages), or participate in any sports on the Sunday. Of course, tobacco and alcohol were forbidden for all my friends, but the smoking prohibition—which was absolute in my family and was especially serious to Daddy—was considered primarily a matter of age, rather than a sin in itself, for most of the others.

Wallace Murphree

As I progressed through grade school I came to feel more and more left out as my classmates would go to the local theatre on Saturday and then talk about the movie for the next week—for I didn't know what the inside of a theatre looked like and had no idea who Roy Rogers or Gene Autry was. And as I grew older I felt further marginalized because the "in-things" the others were doing were all prohibited for me. For example, when football became the rage (in the eighth grade) I disparately wished I could participate; however, since I was not even allowed to attend the games I was also left out as the rest of the class—often including the teacher—discussed each week's contest play by play. And the same was the case for many, if not most, of the other social activities of my class peers. So, to some degree, at least, I lived in perpetual humiliation in the presence my classmates—whose approval and acceptance I perhaps desired pathologically during that period.

I was generally frustrated with my parents because of the restrictions and became sullen and angry from time to time; but down deep I knew I really couldn't blame them. Instead, I fully believed my desire to be included in these worldly affairs to be the lust of my own fallen nature and, hence, something that it was my duty to resist. And I certainly did intend to resist such desire in the long run in order to keep from going to hell. But, at the time I couldn't help but feel that life was passing me by while I didn't even know what was going on.

So as an early teenager I began breaking the rules I could get by with—that is, I began actively "sneaking and sinning"—in search of the worldly pleasures I was missing out on. Of course, like every other sinner, I didn't intend to be wayward forever. In fact, I didn't plan to remain astray very long, for I took to heart the Camp Meeting evangelists' warning of how insidious the treacherous slope of sin is, and how easy it is to keep postponing the return forever. But I was determined to return; so during this period I continued to pray every night, and sometimes during the day, to remind both God and myself that my digression was only temporary and that my long-range intention was that of a life committed to Christ.

From Faith to Doubt...and Life as a Failed Believer

But even given my sure resolve to return, the venture seemed to be fraught with two very horrible dangers. One was that I might suffer an untimely death before I returned and then go to hell forever—and the cases of such I had heard from Camp Meeting evangelists made any excursion into sin indescribably scary. So, to my mind this was taking an awful risk with my eternal soul and I am sure the fear deterred me from straying for some time. But after a while I became willing to take the chance, even while believing it was absolutely irrational to do so.

The other danger was the possibility that I should commit "the unpardonable sin" and, hence, then be unable to be forgiven. And a special problem with this possibility was that no one knew for sure which sin was the unpardonable one, although everyone agreed that it wasn't what we would ordinarily think of as the "worst sin," such as murder or rape. However, the view most prevalent at Camp Meeting, and the one I assumed to be correct, was that it was the "sin of unbelief."

The evidence for this theory was that while there are many documented cases of people reared as atheists who later became believers, there are no known cases of Christians who became atheists and then later returned to Christianity. And the explanation was that while Christians may backslide and sin—even commit murder or rape—they may then earnestly repent and receive forgiveness from God. However, when the erstwhile Christian falls into a state of unbelief he or she no longer considers the unbelief to be a sin, and this makes earnest repentance for it impossible. So, it is not that God would refuse to forgive such disloyalty if he were asked; rather, the sin is unpardonable because it is impossible for such a sinner to ask a God (who is thought not to exist) for forgiveness (for something not thought to be a sin).

At first I assumed I would have no difficulty on this issue. However, after a few months astray—and out of the blue—I remembered the doubt my earlier consideration of the Eskimo boy's religion had prompted. Although that was nearly half a lifetime before, it now seemed very important again. And as I reconsidered it I realized I never did get it settled but, instead, I had just quit thinking about it after telling myself my parents would have protected me from any false religious doctrines.

So I began to wonder whether I really believed after all, or if I was simply refusing to let go of a child's fairy tale by continuing my daily prayers. In fact, I think the very fear of doubting—i.e., the fear of committing the unpardonable sin—became so strong for a while that I could not pray, affirm the Apostles' Creed in church, or read the Bible without wondering if I really believed that Christianity was true.

However, one Sunday evening it seemed the sermon at our home church must have been meant specifically for me. The pastor made the distinction between "being tempted to doubt" and "actually doubting." Accordingly, he claimed Satan tempts most, if not all, believers to doubt at some time or other; but, he claimed, *it is not a sin to be tempted to doubt.* Rather, the sin occurs if one yields to that temptation and actually accepts and assents to the unbelief.

I was very glad to see this distinction; subsequently whenever I felt the compulsion to wonder whether I really believed I would simply repeat "I believe" again and again—out loud if I was by myself—until my attention was diverted and I would find myself thinking about something else. (I would picture the diverted thought as a sign that Satan had given up on the temptation for the time being.) Furthermore, once this strategy began working then the compulsion to wonder grew weaker and rarer, and finally practically faded away.

As it turned out, I was rather disappointed in the pleasures of the world. I distinctly remember drinking my first Coca Cola—: it was in the final week of my eighth grade. I got the coke, and then swaggered around at the end-of-the-year picnic so everyone could see me with it. (Of course, no one noticed.) But then when I took my first gulp it

From Faith to Doubt...and Life as a Failed Believer

burned my throat so terribly that I couldn't see how anyone would like it. Also, cigarettes and "homebrew" (it was a dry county) which I soon tried just made me sick at first. And even after I was addicted to nicotine and came to tolerate alcohol it didn't seem that I was having that much more fun than my unrebellious sister and brothers. I think I questioned whether the Christians had misrepresented the pleasures of worldliness, but I concluded that my rather bland experience of it was consistent with the workings of the devil. That is, I concluded that since I already was offering no resistance to the fun-sin-opportunities he provided, Satan simply had no reason to reward me with much pleasure for committing them.

I set a date some months in advance when I planned to rededicate my life to Christ and get "reclaimed"—: I planned to respond to the first invitation given at Camp Meeting the next summer, and to stay at the altar until I had "prayed through." That is, I planned to stay and pray until I was assured I had been forgiven. However, I was now not certain I knew how to get forgiven or, if I was forgiven, how to know that I was. I had heard of cases when sinners who responded to the invitation would actually leave the altar unforgiven—before they "prayed through." Presumably they had some secret sin that, unconsciously, they were unwilling to give up. So, I wondered how to tell whether, after I confessed and repented, I had actually given up all my secret sins that I might be unaware of. I was especially concerned since I "knew" my whole life rightfully belonged to God, but my plan had been to cheat him out of part of it, so to speak. So, if he forgave me when I repented according to my own timetable, then perhaps he would be endorsing my unholy plan. Indeed, if I repented according to my own pre-established timetable, it seemed questionable if it could be genuine repentance at all. Rather, it seemed that genuine repentance had to carry remorse for having strayed, whereas such pre-scheduled repentance would still be carrying out (the final step in) my own sinful plan. Also, to be forgiven one had to believe that he or she was forgiven, and I was afraid I wouldn't be able to do that while I had these questions. So, I wondered if I, along with Satan's generous help, had simply outsmarted myself in this attempt to enjoy worldly pleasure for a season and then return for eternal life also. I knew any attempt to outwit God had to be self-defeating, but now it occurred to me that this might be precisely what I had been trying to do—although I hadn't thought of it as being so before.

I responded to the first invitation that summer, and took all these questions and fears to the altar with me. I couldn't understand them all, and I didn't know where they left me standing in God's sight—for God saw things as they really were. But at the time I felt strongly that if I didn't get right with God then and there the situation would surely grow more and more hopeless and I finally would be...*Lost After All.*

I was the only one who responded to the invitation that evening. I knelt at the altar and silently prayed with all my might. I could hear the congregation singing the prayer, "Take Me as I Am," in the background, but it seemed that nothing was happening to me spiritually. Then the evangelist knelt beside me and asked,

"Do you confess your sins to God?"
"Yes."
"Do you believe the Bible?"
"Yes."
"Did you know the Bible says: *If we confess our sins, He is faithful and just to forgive us our sins, and to cleanse us from all unrighteousness (I John 1:9)?*
"Yes."
"Then you must see—you ARE forgiven!"

And I saw! It was so simple!

I stood and faced the congregation, and the evangelist led as we all sang the familiar chorus:

> I'm glad salvation's free,
> I'm glad salvation's free;

From Faith to Doubt...and Life as a Failed Believer

> Salvation's free for you and me,
> I'm glad salvation's free.

To use a phrase I had heard my father use in describing his childhood religious experience, "I felt so light I could fly!" Every hint of doubt had disappeared and I felt certain that I had begun the lifetime of service and commitment to Christ that I always intended. I did not know what it would be—"what he would call me to do"—missionary, pastor, or lay person; but my theme song was "Where He leads me I will follow; I'll go with Him, with Him, all the way."

The elated feeling was transient, as I had been told it would be. However, the change in my outlook was for real and, although the high feeling was soon gone, I continued to be happy thinking of myself as a born-again child of God. I tried to "walk with Christ" by maintaining a constant consciousness of his presence—just like I would be constantly aware of a human friend when one was with me.

Not only did I attempt to stay in his presence all day, but I regularly held my personal devotions each evening after the family devotions were over. I would read at least a chapter in the Bible, rehearse whatever verses I was memorizing, sing a couple of hymns, and pray. However, when I was an overnight guest, or had an overnight guest, I would forego the overt actions and simply sing and pray in silence after I lay down.

I was uncomfortable with the public display of my religion, especially when it was not in a church context, and this caused me some uneasiness. I thought that Christians should not be ashamed, but I knew it would embarrass me to have my personal devotions in the presence of another, even if the other was a Christian. In fact, whenever I prayed publicly in church or prayer meeting—or was even called on to "say grace" over a meal—I often felt more like I was performing for a human audience than actually praying to God.

Also, I was embarrassed to "witness" in an everyday context, or to try to lead my friends to Christ. Of course, I tried to let my "new life" be an example, but I had trouble actually asking classmates if they were saved, ready to die, etc. On the one hand, I knew this could be counterproductive if I became obnoxious, and I had seen some evangelistic types do this; but I felt I was veering on the side of my timidity, and was not witnessing aggressively enough to be effective.

I guess people always harbor a background fear that one of their friends will die unexpectedly, but now this seemed much more pressing to me—: What if an unsaved friend whom I have not tried to win to Christ dies in an accident?

My fear was not that my friend's "blood would be on my hands," as some evangelists preached. Rather, my fear was just that he or she would go to eternal suffering. So, it seemed clear that I owed it to my friends, as well as to any stranger I met, to do anything I could that might help prevent this. And the more I pondered the clearer it seemed that the only worthwhile goal in this life is staying in God's will by trying to lead as many sinners to Christ as possible. Any and every other activity—whether going to school, working in the field, or whatever—was justified only to the extent that it subserved this final end, directly or in the long run.

I prayed for the wisdom that would discern between being too shy and too aggressive in my testimony, and the strength act on that wisdom. After a while I think I did become somewhat more assertive.

***

For quite a few years my father was principal of a country school that went from the first through the tenth grades, and this is where I attended for my seventh, ninth and tenth grades. Prior to my conversion experience I fell in love with Martha, who was a grade behind me there. I was in the ninth and our two classes took a bus trip to Montgomery to observe the state legislature in action, and I took

From Faith to Doubt...and Life as a Failed Believer

the aisle seat next to her on our return trip that evening. The seats faced forward and rearward in an alternating fashion so as to form sets of near secluded cubicles with places for four passengers each.

Martha's and my seat was turned forward, and we sat face to face with two of her friends whose seat was turned around. The four of us then talked, and laughed, and sang all the way back home—and the three-hour trip passed in what seemed hardly any time at all. We could see the sun on the Montgomery horizon as we left, and I believe it had not yet grown dark before I was overwhelmed by the magic of the setting and my feelings for Martha had become overpowering. Then, out on the country highway, every time the bus rounded one side of a curve the full moon illuminated her profile, and I remember thinking that only an angel could be that lovely.

Although the school was small, the social dynamics were such that it was difficult for me to have anything more than occasional and casual contact with her after that. However, for the rest of the year I looked forward to each day in hopes of an opportunity to speak to her, or receive a smile from her. I had no chance to see her during the following summer months at all; however, I remained obsessed with the thoughts of her, and finally got the courage to write—and I worked on the letter for several days before I finally mailed it. But she didn't respond and this, of course, made the prospects of seeing her in the fall more disquieting. (Years later she was surprised to hear I had written, and said she didn't receive a letter from me that summer.)

Indeed, the entire following school year provided only limited opportunity for me even to speak to her in passing, much less any opening for the initiation of a continued dialogue. Furthermore, I heard that she now had a boyfriend in the larger town south of Wedowee where her father worked. In addition, as this was the year I had strayed into worldly pleasure, my reputation for being rebellious and trouble for my parents would probably have preempted any relationship that might have developed otherwise, since she was a very devout Christian.

However, my Camp Meeting experience followed that school year and, later on that summer, I attended the ten-day gospel "singing school" held at the country school gymnasium. Quite a few schoolmates attended as well—including Martha and also the two of her friends who sat with us on that trip back from Montgomery the year before. Again it was a magical time for me, and there social interaction came natural and easy. Usually several of us would come early and gather around the piano and practice our parts. Most agreed that I was the best bass singer of the students, so I was included in several combinations as we divided into quartets.

By then I had my driver's license, so during the rest of the summer and the following year Martha and I attended several gospel singings and evening school functions together. We sang, recited poetry, discussed religion, and talked about our future on these dates. I was earnestly in love with her, but to her I was just a "good friend," and she continued to see her boyfriend from the larger town. But she was my date to the (danceless) junior-senior prom at my high school in Wedowee, and I still treasure the photograph from that evening.

Over this period I think my addiction to nicotine had been completely broken, although the allure of cigarettes remained as a forbidden pleasure. Then one day I found myself alone where a single cigarette had been left. I resisted the temptation for an hour or more, I guess; and then I succumbed to it. My remorse was profound, and I felt totally unworthy of the forgiveness I earnestly prayed for. But I began anew, resolving with all the strength I knew how to muster that this would be a lone and singular aberration. However, in a few weeks an uncannily similar opportunity presented itself, and this time I offered even less resistance, and my remorse was neither as immediate nor as profound. And my religious life spiraled downward as I came to yield increasingly quicker to smoking opportunities, and to enjoy progressively wilder indiscretions while I was astray—and then go

From Faith to Doubt...and Life as a Failed Believer

longer and longer before I would "re-repent." I became very disgusted with myself but, try as I might, it seemed I couldn't get my resolutions to stick, and my baser self had developed quite a skill in Methodist art of backsliding!

Upon finishing the tenth grade, Martha transferred to the city school south of Wedowee where she was quite popular, and certainly didn't need me for a social contact. Furthermore, because of my new round of indiscretions she broke our relationship off altogether.

Then, upon finishing high school I followed Sarah and Tal to Asbury College near Lexington, KY. It was a religious school whose outlook was endorsed by our parents. Its rules prohibited most everything prohibited in my home environment, and its social policies were even much more restrictive. Its president had been an evangelist at Camp Meeting the summer before I went to the altar, and campus life overall had a Camp Meeting feeling to it. For example, there were three mandatory chapel services each week, classes always opened with a devotional and prayer, and it was not unusual for "spontaneous revivals" to break out.

With its strict rules and evangelical student body, I hoped the new environment would bolster the feeble re-repentance and re-resolution I made when I entered. But the re-backsliding continued; in fact, it became a vicious cycle, from which there seemed to be no way of escape—except to re-repent after each relapse. At the heart of the problem (at least, superficially) was my inability to quite smoking. I would pray for forgiveness, and claim it, and quit smoking for three or four days, or a week. But then I would always light up again. Although I hid my smoking as much as I could, I was eventually suspected of such and asked not to return to school following my second quarter there.

After a couple of months at home I volunteered for the army. My idea was to break out of the vicious cycle by *quitting* quitting smoking and re-repenting—at least until it would cease to be such an ordinary affair for me. In addition, although I was aware of the rigorous military requirements, I was also attracted by the two years of uncensored worldly pleasure the army would allow me to pursue. So the ploy was a replay of my earlier excursion into the worldliness, although this time it was to be for a longer period. And as I had done earlier, I set the time in advance (after I was to be released from active duty) when I would finally permanently turn away from a life of sin.

I wrote Martha at her home address before returning to Wedowee on Christmas leave; I had just finished basic training and asked if I could see her before I was transferred to Germany. She had just finished her first semester at Southern Union, the two-year college in the county, and my letter arrived just as she returned home. In response, she invited me to join her and her family on their annual caroling excursion through their rural neighborhood.

I enjoyed this time with her and her family immensely. Her younger sister took the opportunity to fill me in some on her past that I had missed—including that she was crowned Homecoming Queen in her high school when I was at Asbury. I relished each moment of this evening, realizing that this might be our last outing ever. When the course was finished, I gazed into her moonlit face for a parting image, and I asked—and received—permission to write her while I was away.

I was chaplain's assistant during my stint in Germany. I tried to do the job well, but the religion I found there was not at all what I understood Christianity to be. In fact, they all seemed to be just "nominal Christians," rather than born-again defenders of the faith. But, of course, I didn't mind, especially since I—a backslidden sinner—was allowed to smoke as I worked in the office, and my evening carousing went uncensored.

During this time both Mother and Daddy wrote regularly. Mother wrote more frequently, but Daddy's letters were usually longer. Once

From Faith to Doubt...and Life as a Failed Believer

Daddy sent a multi-page poem he had written to me, which left me in tears. Also my siblings would write from time to time, and my brother just younger sent a very touching poem he had written upon the death of our old family dog. Also, they sent a tape once—which was quite a hi-tech thing to do for the times—on which each family member had spoken to me, and which also contained a regular evening devotions that, along with singing and scripture, included their prayers for me.

Martha also answered my letters to her, but the responses came slower and slower throughout the months. They were friendly and warm but the enthusiasm always seemed measured to make sure I didn't draw any false hope from what she said. One letter included newspaper clippings announcing that she had been crowned Miss Southern Union during her second year at the college.

She was so modest I knew it wasn't easy for her to tell me about this honor. In fact, she was so modest that I knew she did not actively seek it, or the earlier homecoming honor in high school, for that matter. So I could only conclude that everyone else had now discovered the loveliness that had charmed me for so long, and I felt sure that this even further diminished whatever remaining chances I might have had to win her heart.

Earlier I had dared to believe that God willed Martha and me for each other, but as my time passed in Germany her letters seemed to indicate a progression in her life that held no significant place for me. I didn't think of this as God's punishment for my sins, at least not in a vindictive way; rather, I pictured it as my having removed myself from his ideal plan by turning away from what I knew to be right. Of course, I still hoped and dreamed of a future with Martha, but I acquiesced in the intention to remain as close and true a friend as the forthcoming opportunities would allow.

Throughout the months in Germany I never lost sight of my resolve to return to Christianity when my active military duty was over. I prayed

Wallace Murphree

each day that I would have the strength and courage to surrender myself completely to God's will at that time.

As I analyzed it, the big stumbling block in my religious life all along had been my smoking. I would always pray for forgiveness and, feeling powerless to quit on my own, I would ask God for strength to implement my resolution; but the resolutions still never held. I concluded it must be that I did have strength to quit on my own after all, and that I must do this as a precondition for forgiveness—for otherwise, it was like asking God to quit smoking for me. This was probably "bad Camp Meeting theology," but maybe it was pretty good psychology since I decided to quit "on my own" beginning my final month on active duty and for that last month I simply did not smoke at all. This was the longest I had gone without smoking since I yielded to that lone cigarette over three years earlier; and since my smoking had become progressively heavier in the army, I had done it from the peak of my nicotine addiction.

With this success I felt optimistic about my prospects of becoming a stable and committed Christian. Of course, I knew better than to think that "now I deserve to be forgiven" or that "hereafter I will be beyond serious temptation." But I did feel good about myself in that one respect; and, confident that he would accept me back, I was anxious to return for good to the loving God I had forsaken.

After the two years in the army I was released from active duty. Then, when I had been home a few days I took my Bible into the solitude of the woods there on the farm, and spent the afternoon with the scriptures, in meditation and prayer. I relived how it felt to believe that Jesus was walking with me as my constant companion, and then how I pictured him as a friend whom I had betrayed, and then as one in whose presence I no longer delighted and, finally, as a stranger. Now I earnestly invited him back into my life, and promised in unqualified sincerity never to forsake him again. As I walked back home in the beauty of that evening, I became overwhelmed with the assurance that he had indeed returned.

From Faith to Doubt...and Life as a Failed Believer

***

Martha didn't have the funds to continue school after she finished Southern Union and, not wanting to strain her parents' resources, she took what was agreed to be a yearlong job as a secretary in the office of the county superintendant of education to earn the tuition she needed. That office was located in the courthouse in Wedowee, which is also where drivers' licenses were issued and renewed.

When I went inside the courthouse to get my license renewed my presiding thought was that Martha was there too. I remember thinking that after being a half-world apart for so long, I was now nearly as close to her as I had been when we went caroling a year and a half earlier. Still, she seemed so far away, for I dared not bother her at her job. In fact, she never answered my last letter from Germany, and I feared she didn't care to see me now that I had returned. But, as when we were in junior high school, I had hoped I might at least catch a glimpse of her while I had the valid reason for being in the courthouse.

I lingered a bit at the water fountain after my business was done when, to my near disbelief, Martha emerged from her office down the hall and came in my direction. The smile that beamed across her face when she recognized who I was gave me all the reason I needed to dream again. Her errand didn't allow her much time to talk but, what was better, she told me it would be all right to phone her at work.

I guess it was lucky for me that her class of friends from high school and college had all graduated and gone their own ways, since this probably made it easier for us to "pick up where we left off" when we were seeing each other before. At least, she seemed happy to spend time with an old friend, and I was delighted to be considered even that. Then, as time passed we grew closer, just as I had dreamed we would. We even talked of marriage.

Wallace Murphree

I was readmitted to Asbury College for the winter quarter, and I convinced her to join me there when she finished her year in the superintendant's office. In the meantime, we stayed in contact by mail, since I didn't have easy access to a telephone on campus.

Chapter 3 Facing the Question

Before I began the downward spiral that landed me in the army I had felt God was calling me to follow my grandfather and father—and now my older brother, Tal—into the ministry, so when I was readmitted to Asbury I declared a pre-ministerial major. The religious atmosphere of the school helped strengthen my commitment to Christ, and its strict regulations helped keep me shielded from worldly temptations. After about a year an opportunity opened up for me to become a student pastor of a small "mission" twenty or so miles from campus, and I felt it was God's will that I should accept. The average attendance was about fifteen—that is, if I would provide transportation for some of them.

I found preparing sermons and spending Sundays at the mission to be a very demanding addition to my fulltime load as a student; but I felt I was in the center of God's will, and I wanted the rest of my life to be so lived. I truly cared for the people of the mission, and I enjoyed the discussion and fellowship with the other students who would come along each week to teach Sunday school and help with the music. I felt the group was especially blessed, and I was very proud, when Tal held a revival meeting for us; and, I was overjoyed with Martha's participation in the ministry. It seemed so obvious that she was "meant to be" a pastor's wife!

Perhaps the most fervent member of the little church was a middle-aged woman who, along with her teenage daughter, needed my transportation each Sunday. Her husband was an atheist tobacco farmer, and rumored to be a bootlegger. At any rate, he would have nothing to do with the mission, which—under the aegis of Asbury—held atheism, tobacco, and alcohol to be important sins. In fact, he would not even take his wife or daughter to the services and he and the two nearly grown sons were openly hostile if they were home when I came for or delivered the mother and daughter. I was literally afraid of them, but the mother assured me they would not harm me physically. She was very kind, and I felt extremely sorry for her— trying so hard to rear her daughter right, after she saw herself as having failed with her sons. As it turned out, it was my inability to minister to the daughter that produced a crisis which, I think, was the ultimate turning point in my religious life.

One morning before Sunday school the daughter whispered that she wanted to talk to me in private. I asked one of my college friends to engage the mother after church, and the daughter and I went to a far corner. She said something like this:

> I love both my mother and my daddy, and I believe they both want what's best for me. My daddy says there is no God, and that he's trying to keep me from growing up to be superstitious like my mother. My mother says there is a God, a heaven and a hell, and she wants me to be saved, and be good, so I'll go to heaven. I don't want to grow up and be mean like my brothers; but I don't want to be superstitious either—and I know my mother is superstitious about some things. It's just that I don't know about religion. But neither my mother or daddy even went to high school and you are in college, so you must know better than they do about what's a superstition and what's really the truth—and I don't believe you'd lie to me. So, I want to know if you know *for sure* that the Bible and religion is true.

If this had been posed by someone I perceived to be in a less precarious situation, I might not have been so troubled by it. But, instead, I saw it as an ingenuous question demanding a straightforward answer that would (or at least, could) have everlasting consequences for this precious life. For her eternal sake, I desperately thought I needed to be able to answer honestly, "Yes, I know *for sure*." But I was unable to do that.

From Faith to Doubt...and Life as a Failed Believer

In fact, I don't remember how I did respond, but I remember vividly how I felt—: I felt like a charlatan who had just been found out. Also, I vividly remember feeling on the spot that I had to leave the appointment until my faith was sufficiently grounded to minister in such crises.

At my request, the college organization sent another student pastor the next week, and I never returned to the chapel, nor spoke again to the girl or her mother.

After all this time, I still feel very bad about deserting her so. Of course, that was not my intention. I assumed, rather, that after a few weeks of study and soul-searching I would be able to return, and honestly tell her that I knew for sure. Indeed, I looked forward to the time with great anticipation. But that's not the way things happened.

It didn't occur to me on the spot, but soon it dawned on me that the problem I confronted that day was the resurrection of, or an extension of, the old problem I had with the Eskimo boy's religion. Now I wondered what I would have come to believe if I, like the mission girl, had had one parent who was a Christian and one who was an atheist. Once I realized I couldn't say, it seemed clear that my faith had been faith in my parents, rather than in God, all along. Moreover, it also seemed clear that I had no right to preach Christianity to others unless I had good reason to accept it under such a circumstance as that. And it was also clear that I would not find a good reason by simply repeating "I believe, I believe, I believe..."

And by the way, the mission girl's appeal to the few years of formal education I had beyond that of her parents exposed how irrelevant my earlier justification that appealed to my parents' education was; and, by the same token, it exposed how wrong-headed it would be for me to ground my faith in what the Camp Meeting evangelists or professors at the college might claim to know.

Wallace Murphree

At the end of the quarter I dropped out of school to work and Martha and I got married as we had planned. During this period I still clung fast to Christianity and maintained my daily devotions. But my religion lost its evangelistic zeal when I admitted to myself I didn't know for sure that it was true. Also, during this time I told myself that, having not smoked for so long, I should now be able to have a cigarette with coworkers during breaks without becoming addicted again. But surely I knew better deep down.

When the weather interrupted my job in construction, I took another in a small factory in Lexington. It turned out that the boss there had completed seminary before he left the church and went into business. From time to time three or four of us would stop by a bar after work and discuss our favorite topics—: University of Kentucky basketball and religion. It was in these discussions that I learned the academic discipline of philosophy actually dealt with the question of whether God exists. I was very excited to learn this, although I recall being embarrassed that I didn't know it already.

Incidentally, one afternoon I stopped in the bar alone. I ordered a beer and lit a cigarette, and soon two boisterous young men began looking my way and laughing as they talked. Then they came and seated themselves across the booth from me, and I recognized them—: they were the older brothers of the girl from the mission. They announced that their mother and sister had always wondered "whatever happened to that preacher-boy," and they couldn't wait to tell them that they had found me. Then one of them ordered pack of cigarettes for me and the other ordered me another beer because, they mocked, "...their mother would sure want them to be friendly to me."

They roared in laughter as I got up and left.

The following spring Martha finished college and Scott was born. Later that summer we sold the trailer we had been buying and moved back to Alabama, where Martha got a job as a social worker and I was admitted to the University of Montevallo. We moved our membership

From Faith to Doubt...and Life as a Failed Believer

to the Methodist church there whose pastor, incidentally, was a childhood friend of my father's.

I enrolled in three philosophy courses my first semester, and was immediately captivated by the field of study generally. But the class in philosophy of religion was especially enticing, because it directly addressed the issue as to whether there are sound reasons for believing that the God of theism—i.e., an omnipotent (all powerful), omniscient (all knowing), and omnibenevolent (perfectly good) being—exists.

We studied the traditional arguments for and against the existence of God (which are summarized in the next chapter), and each seemed very compelling when it was presented. However, the criticisms of each that followed also seemed very powerful, as then did the responses to the criticisms—and on and on. One thing I found so exhilarating was the academic atmosphere in which students could criticize, question, and follow an idea wherever it led without fear being thought irreverent. Indeed, students were encouraged to do this. But the professor was not trying to undermine religious faith; in fact, he was a lay Methodist minister himself, and the author of the text he had chosen for the course was a renowned religious thinker. But inherent in the orientation was the belief that honest inquiry demands a fair consideration of both sides of any issue and, as a correlate, that no philosophical belief is so cherished, and no faith so sacred, as to make it exempt from impartial scrutiny.

Having transferred to Montevallo late in my college career, I didn't have time to complete the major in philosophy before I was able to graduate; so I accepted a philosophy minor instead, and this allowed me to enter graduate school in philosophy at Vanderbilt.

Originally I wanted to concentrate my studies on the question of God's existence, but that was very narrow and it became clear that other issues in the discipline were also pertinent to the faith that I questioned. So to get a broader perspective I took the courses I needed from the Divinity School to get a minor in theology and I elected to write my dissertation on "the mind-body problem"—which is relevant for the question of eternal life.

My outlook fluctuated some during the first semesters at Vanderbilt but its overall direction tended away from Christianity, although I guess I was not aware of it as it was happening; at least, I didn't admit it to myself at first. I mentioned above that I never ceased to pray when I had drifted into sin earlier; also I continued to pray regularly through college and into graduate school. In fact, I tried to imagine how it would feel to go to bed that first night without praying, if I ever should become convinced that there was no God. I thought it would have to be such an important, life-changing moment that I would probably be unable to sleep. But that's not how it happened. Rather, one night as I lay down I suddenly realized that I hadn't prayed in the past several days. I had *forgotten* to pray! And, although I have "said grace" over a meal a few times since when I couldn't decline without excessive awkwardness, I have never actually tried to pray again. In fact, from then on, the act of seriously praying to the God of my childhood has seemed as alien—as impossible for me to do—as would the act of seriously praying to some unknown Hindu god. This is not to say that I haven't felt the need to call out to "whatever gods there may be," or "to God if there be a God," as one might call out into the night in hopes that someone is there. But suddenly it felt like I no longer knew how to pray "in earnest," as I always had before.

Kate was born in my last year at Vanderbilt. From there the four of us moved to Starkville, Mississippi, where I was appointed to the faculty in the newly formed Department of Philosophy and Religion at Mississippi State University.

My teaching duties at Mississippi State typically required me to offer three or four classes a semester. Of these, at least one would be a section of Introduction to Philosophy and one would be an upper division course. In the introductory class I always elected to include a

From Faith to Doubt...and Life as a Failed Believer

component in philosophy of religion, where traditional arguments for and against the existence of God were presented and criticized in a survey fashion; and ordinarily, every fourth semester I taught Philosophy of Religion as my upper division course. There we considered the traditional arguments and their criticisms in much greater depth, and looked at a variety of wider issues as the schedule allowed.

Each time through the Philosophy of Religion course I tried to look at the subject matter with fresh eyes, and each time through it seemed I always did get new insights. But pretty early in my teaching career I became convinced that the traditional arguments fail to furnish a satisfactory justification either for theism or for atheism, and each subsequent semester seemed to confirm it. Indeed, I had practically reached that conclusion before I left graduate school.

So, although there are both theists and atheists who present testimonials to the contrary, I did not find the answer to my religious doubts in philosophy. I'm sure the Camp Meeting evangelists—and Asbury professors and, certainly, my parents—would have told me to begin with that I would not find it there. In fact, I suppose they tried to.

In the next chapter I present a summary of these traditional arguments. Again these are attempted proofs for the existence or nonexistence of God that have emerged though the centuries. I have studied and have taught these over the years and what I am reporting is that if—like the mission girl—one of my parents had been an atheist and the other a believer, I would not have been able to determine which was correct on the basis of these attempted proofs.

Chapter 4 Philosophical Arguments

Perhaps there is no end to number of arguments that might be constructed for or against the existence of God. However, the four arguments for, and one argument against, that are sketched below are the ones most widely considered in philosophy.

While I think the gist of each can be captured in a summary, it would be a grave misconception to conclude that "this is all there is to it" for any one of them. Rather, volumes have been written and many, many genius-hours have been devoted to each in the history of Western thought, and contributions that address their presuppositions, implications, and general relevance continue to accumulate.

In addition, standard criticisms of and responses to the arguments have evolved, and criticisms of the criticisms and responses to the responses continue to be forthcoming as these conversations span the centuries.

So I shall not attempt a summary of the criticisms. Instead, readers can well supply their own criticisms, or—if they feel an argument is cogent—they might ask themselves what a thinker of the opposite persuasion might find unacceptable about it. However, I have advanced one criticism that I feel is damaging to all the arguments; and, since I want to refer to it later, I shall present it to conclude the chapter.

The Teleological Argument

Also called "The Argument from Design," the teleological argument is quite popular in common sense. It contends that the intricate order in the natural world is of such complexity that there must exist a supernatural intelligence—i.e., a God—who arranged it so.

From Faith to Doubt...and Life as a Failed Believer

Although renditions of this argument were advanced by ancient Greek philosophers, perhaps the most popular version was crafted by William Paley [1743-1805] where he compares the human eye to a watch. There he reasons that if the intricate workings of the watch rightly lead us to believe that it was designed by some intelligence (rather than the result of mere chance happenings of natural forces), then when we examine the immeasurably more intricate workings of the human eye we are also right to conclude that it also was designed by some intelligence. Indeed, here the justification for our conclusion is many times stronger, and the designer inferred must be a most Superior Intelligence, or God.

Of course, other examples in nature serve just as well. For example, Joyce Kilmer's "Trees," is a poetic statement of this argument. Its opening and closing couplets are:

> I think that I shall never see
> A poem lovely as a tree.
> ....
> Poems are made by fools like me
> But only God can make a tree.

That is, if when we see a poem we are justified in believing that it was composed by an intelligent designer—by a poet, rather than by monkeys in a typing classroom—we are much more justified in believing there was an Intelligent Designer when we see a tree, because the design in a tree is so much more advanced than the design in a poem. Every old fool has made a poem, but no one has ever a tree.

And while Darwin's theory of natural selection may seem to weaken the impact of the human eye or tree example, supporters of the argument contend that the more science progresses, the ever heightened intricacy of the design that is revealed makes it more and more irrational to suppose it all just fell in place by sheer chance.

Along these lines, a passage from the Old Testament reads: "The heavens declare the glory of God, and the firmament showeth his handiwork"; [Psalms 19:1][2] that is, the design in the universe is said to be the "signature" of God. Incidentally, one of Tal's books employs this type of reasoning; it is entitled *Autographed by God.*[3]

The Cosmological Argument

Also known as the "First Cause Argument," the cosmological argument, like the teleological argument, is well established in common sense. It contends that the natural world cannot be explained by anything in it and concludes that there must therefore be a God "outside" of it that is responsible for it. The common sense expression of it is often something like, "There has to be someone—i.e., God—who created everything."

Although versions of this argument were also given by ancient Greek philosophers—most notably by Aristotle [384-322 BCE]—its classical Christian rendition was given by St. Thomas Aquinas [1225-1274] after lost portions of Aristotle's philosophy had been reintroduced to the Western tradition.

St. Thomas notes that in the natural world there are series of events in which each later member follows from an earlier member—as today we might picture how the falling of any one domino in a series was preceded and caused by the falling of its neighbor. And such is the

---

[2] All Biblical references are to the King James Version.
[3] Jon Tal Murphree, *Autographed by God: A Reasoned Case For Christianity* (University Park IA: Vennard College, 2006)

From Faith to Doubt...and Life as a Failed Believer

case for all motion in the world, for nothing moves itself but, rather, is always set in motion by the preceding motion of something else. And, in general, this is the case for each cause-and-effect series in the world.

However, no series of previous events can "go back forever." That is, no current series can have come from forever ago, for then an infinite number of instances would have already occurred—which is an impossibility. Instead, like the human hand that pushed the first domino, there has to be some outside force that initiated the world's activities in the beginning. That is, there has to be an Unmoved Mover or Uncaused Cause outside of the series; i.e., there has to exist a God.

Since causes and motions are temporal concepts, perhaps underlying this reasoning is the idea that an infinite amount of time can never pass. That is, an infinite number of years (days, hours, or any unit of time) is precisely the amount that can never, never pass; instead, as each new year is added to the last the sum will always be a finite number—forever. But the atheist who claims that the world has always existed is saying that an infinite number of years has *already* passed, which is something which cannot have happened.

So since this is impossible, one must say instead that time, itself, began some finite number of years ago, and that its creator is a being that is "outside of time"; i.e., one must say there exists a God that is timeless and eternal.

But in addition to asking what must have existed in the beginning in order to account for causes, motion, and time in the present, some thinkers contend an even stronger version of this general type of reasoning would begin by asking what, *at any given time*, sustains the natural world, and "keeps it existing." That is, at any given moment the existence of one thing in the natural world depends on something outside it, and the existence of it also depends on something outside it, and so on and on. And since this is true for everything in the

37

natural world, then the natural world as a whole must be dependent on something beyond it, for otherwise it would be "holding itself up by its own bootstraps." And this being beyond the natural world has to be an independent and self-sustaining being (i.e., God), for otherwise it, along with the natural world whose existence depends on it, would both come crashing down.

Dependent beings are usually called "contingent" beings in this context, and independent, self-sustaining beings are called "necessary" beings. So, in summary, this version of the argument contends that since the natural world is composed of contingent beings, there must be a supernatural world in which a necessary being (i.e., God) exists.

The Ontological Argument

The ontological argument is not often, if ever, found in common sense; also, it was not advanced by the ancient Greek thinkers, although in retrospect it seems it was implicit in the philosophy of Plato [427-347 BCE] all along. In fact, St. Augustine [354-430 CE], whose Christianity was conceptualized through Plato's thought, came close to giving the argument; but it was St. Anselm [1033-1109]— also a Platonist—who finally worked it out several centuries later.

I think of it as the most enigmatic of the traditional arguments by far. I remember that I had trouble understanding it at first; and through the years I have had exasperated students throw up their hands and pronounce it to be just a word game. However, if it were, it would have been exposed as such a long time ago. Instead, many contemporary thinkers contend that recent developments in "modal logic" have shown Anselm's insights to be way ahead of his time.

Unlike the cosmological and teleological arguments which proceed from observations about the natural world to the conclusion that God exists, the ontological argument simply looks at the *idea* of God and

From Faith to Doubt...and Life as a Failed Believer

argues that from the proper understanding of this idea one can tell that God does indeed exist.

Of course, from the idea of most things we can't tell whether they exist, and so we have to investigate the world to see if they do. But the proponents of this argument hold that this is not the case for everything. For example, we know without looking that square circles don't exist; that is, we don't have to investigate to see if there are any, for we know by understanding "square" and "circle" that square circles *can't* exist. In a similar vein, proponents of the ontological argument contend that when we understand the idea of God properly we see that such a being does exist, because he *has to* exist. That is, as the idea of a square circle is the idea of something that cannot exist, the idea of God is the idea of something that cannot *not*-exist. Of course, this can only be seen if one has an adequate concept of God for, of course, one can doubt the existence of an old man in the sky.

Furthermore, it also seems clear that the existence of an omnipotent, omniscient, and omnibenevolent being can also be doubted just as easily—if these are the only properties the being has. Of course, St. Anselm holds that God does have these three properties but he thinks the concept of God also contains much more.

His definition is:

> God is that than which nothing greater can be conceived,

or equivalently,

> God is that than which nothing greater is possible,

or again,

> God is that which nothing can possibly be greater than.

Now, "that which nothing can possibly be greater than" is that which possesses every "great-making property" to the maximum degree. That is, such a being would have no shortcoming or deficiency whatever; indeed, it could not conceivably be improved upon because it would already be absolutely perfect.

So as this definition is unpacked it is clear that the properties traditionally attributed to God are included in it. That is, since power, knowledge, and goodness are greater than weakness, ignorance, and evil, that which has every great-making property must certainly have these properties. Furthermore, power, knowledge, and goodness *to the maximum degree* are, respectively, omnipotence, omniscience, and omnibenevolence; so, again, Anselm's definition includes these, just as the traditional concept of God does.

But in addition, the full concept of God must include not only these three properties but every other great-making property as well. Of course, there may be some disagreement as to which other properties are great-making ones, but Anselm assumed everyone should agree that existence is to be ranked very high. That is, in the same way we would think an existing dollar to be greater than an imaginary one and an existing friend to be greater than an imaginary one, surely we must conceive an existing God to be greater than an imaginary one. Indeed, a real friend is greater than a make-believe god.

So just as that which has no shortcoming whatever cannot fail to be omnipotent, omniscient, or omnibenevolent, it also cannot fail to be *existent*—if existence is, indeed, also a great-making property. Moreover, it seems clear that "existence to the maximum degree" would be necessary rather than contingent existence, and this insight allows champions of the argument to present it succinctly in modern modal logic (which employs possibility and necessity operators).

Accordingly, proponents of this reasoning contend the belief that God does not exist is a logical error, rather than a mere error of fact.

From Faith to Doubt...and Life as a Failed Believer

The Moral Argument

The Moral Argument claims that God has to exist in order for morality to be intelligible.

There is a version of The Moral Argument which proceeds:

> For there to be moral right and wrong, there must be moral laws to which actions conform or fail to conform; and, for there to be moral laws, there must be a moral Lawgiver, or God. Therefore, if we believe in moral right and wrong, we have to believe there exists a God.

This reasoning only holds, however, for those who subscribe to what is called "the divine command theory" of moral law, viz., the view that "having been commanded by God" is what makes a policy a moral law. But, although this view has some popular support (indeed, I believed it as a young Christian), its acceptance is limited in philosophy and theology.

The version of the argument that receives more attention was offered by Immanuel Kant [1724-1804], who contended that there is a supreme moral law which everyone, even including God, ought to obey. Indeed, to say that God is morally perfect is to say that he always obeys this law.

(This moral law, called The Categorical Imperative, seems close to The Golden Rule, and might be summarized without too much distortion as: "Do unto others as you would rationally have everyone do unto everyone.")

Now, Kant's argument for the existence of God proceeds, first, by noting what he takes to be the obvious truth that "ought implies can." That is, he holds that if we truly ought to do something, then we can do it, and also we can refrain from doing it, for is possible for us to choose either way. And, in general, if something really ought to be, then it can be—i.e., it is possible for it to be, and it is possible for it not to be.

Now we frequently believe it is possible for us to do either of two things, but that we ought to do the one thing when we'd rather do the other. This conflict between duty and self-interest is the situation of moral temptation and, according to Kant, it is only in this circumstance that our actions have moral worth. If we overcome the temptation by choosing to sacrifice what we want in order to do what we ought, then our act is morally good, while if we shun our duty in order to have what we want, our act is morally bad, or sinful. But, on the other hand, when our desire happens to conform to what we ought to do, then our action has no moral value at all.

For example, we ought to tell the truth; but if we also want to tell the truth in this case, then there is no virtue in telling it, because we didn't sacrifice any personal happiness to do it. If fact, in this case we have no free choice since duty and self-interest both motivate us in the same direction. So, for Kant, the morally good life is very difficult for it is the life of resisting temptation which, at each step, requires the free surrendering of what one wants to do for the sake of what one ought to do.

But, still further, Kant holds it to be an obvious truth that happiness should be proportional to moral goodness. That is, it ought to be that evil people are not happy, but that good people are happy—according to how evil or good they are. But this is certainly not the case with human life here on earth. On the one hand, we can factually observe that it is often the wicked who prosper; and on the other hand, we understand that this is the nature of the case, since those who are morally good, i.e., those deserving of happiness, are the very ones who have chosen to forego their happiness in favor of doing their duty.

But, the reasoning continues, since the morally good ought to be happy, then their happiness is possible because "ought implies can."

From Faith to Doubt...and Life as a Failed Believer

But since moral goodness requires surrendering one's happiness in this life, the only venue in which the correlation of moral goodness with happiness is possible is in another life. Moreover, the only way this would be possible in another life would be if there is a being who knows the details of each earthly life and the measure of happiness that each deserves, and also has the power and the will to mete out the happiness accordingly. Such a being would have to have perfect knowledge, power, and justice; i.e., such a being would be God.

Kant doesn't claim that this reasoning proves the existence of God in a theoretical sense; in fact, he holds that God's existence cannot be proved theoretically, and he gives his own criticism of the cosmological, teleological, and ontological arguments. Also, he holds that free will and life after death cannot be proved theoretically; but he claims that these are practical postulates that are rational. That is, he claims we must accept these postulates in order *to make sense out of* our moral duty, for the belief that there is a moral right and wrong finally makes sense only on the further suppositions that there is a God and that human beings have free will and are immortal.

Incidentally, Kant contends that the acceptance of these practical postulates constitute a "rational faith."

***

These four arguments have been the predominant ones in the history of Western philosophy; of course, there have been others, and new ones might be advanced. One argument (or type of argument) we would look at in class from time to time (depending to what anthology we were using) is "the argument from religious experience." That is, there are impressive testimonies from the great mystics through the ages who claim to have met, or to have been in communion with, God. Also, throughout each age similar reports have come from multitudes of ordinary, humble believers. And clearly, if it indeed even one of these reports is true, then God exists.

Wallace Murphree

Other quasi-popular arguments include,

Arguments from answered prayers,
Argument from internal coherence of the scriptures,
Argument from fulfilled prophesy,
Argument from the universality of religious beliefs,
Etc.

The Problem of Evil

Not having a proof for the existence of God need not be an obstacle to faith. However, if there is a successful proof that God does not exist, then that settles the question in favor of atheism, just as any successful proof for the existence of God would settle the question in favor of theism.

Historically, the most influential argument for atheism is the so-called "Problem of Evil." The sense of the argument is that the evil in the world would not have been allowed if there existed a God.

Here the term, *evil*, is used broadly to mean something like "anything that ought not to be," or "anything that it would be our duty to prevent if we could (without causing an equal or greater evil)." That is, if something is really evil, then even an uninvolved passerby would have a duty to prevent it if he or she could without causing an equal or greater evil.

Of course, individuals disagree as to what things really are evil, but that does not matter for this issue. Rather, all that is necessary for the argument is the belief that there exists something or other that ought not to be, whether there is agreement on what it is or not.

So the Problem of Evil has no significance for anyone who thinks everything is just fine. However, most people, at least, believe that evil exists to some degree and, perhaps more importantly, theists believe that its existence is a very grave matter. Indeed, the entire

From Faith to Doubt...and Life as a Failed Believer

redemption scheme in Christianity is cast as the heavenly response to earthly evil.

It is standard to distinguish two logically different versions of this argument. The so-called "deductive version" can be stated as follows (although it is often put in terms of preventing, rather than eradicating, evil):

1. An omnibenevolent being eradicates all evil that it knows about and is able to eradicate.
2. An omniscient being knows about all evil.
3. An omnipotent being is able to eradicate all evil.
4. Not all evil has been eradicated. (I.e., Evil exists.)
5. Therefore, there does not exist an omnipotent, omniscient, and omnibenevolent being. (I.e., Therefore, God does not exist.)

The attempt to justify Christian faith in the face of this problem is called a *theodicy* or a *defense*, and frequently such efforts are designed to show that an omnibenevolent being would be willing to allow some evil after all if it is the only logical way to achieve an even greater good.

Those who advance theodicies or defenses usually distinguish between "moral evil" and "natural evil." Moral evil, or sin, is evil that creatures commit and that they therefore are guilty of, while natural evil is evil that that no one commits and that everyone is innocent of. So, for example, murder is moral evil. That is, it is evil—because a passerby would have had the duty to prevent it if he or she could without causing a greater evil, and it is an evil that the murderer commits and is guilty of. On the other hand, the accidental drowning of a child is natural evil. That is, it is evil—for a passerby would have the duty to save the child if he or she could—and, supposing the guardians were not negligent, it is an evil that no one is guilty of.

Given this distinction, the believer's theory as to why God might allow moral evil can be different from the one proposed to explain why he might allow natural evil. For example, the value of free will is often invoked to explain why God would sometimes allow murder. Certainly God could have prevented every murder by making everyone puppets that were pre-programmed not to kill. However, it could be that free will is such a great good, or causes such a great good, that the overall value of God's creation is enhanced by granting this gift to his creatures, even though its misuse does occasionally result in murder.

But, of course, one cannot blame natural evils on free will. However, the believer might contend the love, compassion, empathy, goodwill, sense of community, etc. that emerges from natural tragedy is so valuable that it outweighs the evil of an occasional drowning in the overall scheme of things.

Proponents of the second or so-called "inductive version" of the argument concede that a perfectly good God might well permit some evil for some greater good, just as these responses to the deductive version claim. But they contend that the amount, intensity, and unjust distribution of evil in the actual world far exceed anything that could reasonably be justified this way. That is, they might concede that a good God could reluctantly permit an occasional murder or drowning; but they contend it stretches one's conscience beyond all credibility to propose that God's creation is better because he did not step in and prevent genocides where millions were murdered, or calm the tsunamis and hurricanes where hundreds of thousands were drowned.

This issue has been central to philosophy of religion throughout Western thought. Indeed, the Greek philosopher, Epicurus [341-270 BCE] argued it long before Christianity appeared on the scene. Furthermore, it has had a prominent place in common sense as well. Although believers are often content to respond that "God moves in mysterious ways" when catastrophe occurs at a distance or calamity

From Faith to Doubt...and Life as a Failed Believer

happens to strangers, they often question how a good God could let it happen to one of his own when disaster strikes nearby.

There were fifteen or so students in my first course in Vanderbilt Divinity School and I think all the rest of them were preparing for the ministry; in fact, several of them were pastoring small churches at the time. The first day of class the professor had us introduce ourselves and then, "as a way to get better acquainted" he asked us to take a few minutes to write down—and then share with the others—the top ten things we would do if our abilities were increased a thousand-fold.

Although there were quite a few projects were named all told, each of our lists contained several items in common, such as:

1. Find a cure for cancer (and other diseases).
2. Create safeguard against highway (and other) accidents.
3. Feed the starving.
4. Provide shelter for the homeless.
5. Stop the war in Viet Nam (which, as it turned out, was only beginning then).
6. Rid the world of nuclear weapons.
7. Etc.

We shared ours lists and spent most of the rest of the session discussing what our top priorities ought to be. Then, to bring the class to a close, the professor gave (something like) the following mini-lecture:

> You will have many challenges as pastors. One of the greatest will be when tragedy strikes the family of a church member. You would have prevented that tragedy if you could have, but you couldn't; the other church members would have prevented it if they could have, but they couldn't. Strangers would have prevented it if they could have, but they couldn't. Now your challenge will be to help the congregation hold onto its trust in a God who could have prevented it, but didn't.

Criticism

As I mentioned above, I do want to summarize one general criticism[4] of the arguments as a group that I have proposed in order to be able to refer to it later: I define "*anti-God*" as an omnipotent, omniscient, and omni*malevent* being," and contend that these arguments for the existence of God support the thesis that anti-God exists just as strongly as they support the view that God exists.

First, if they are successful at all, the Teleological and Cosmological Arguments only establish the existence of an orderer and a creator of the universe. Indeed, it is frequently pointed out that the God of these arguments could well be less than omnipotent, omniscient, and omnibenevolent. Here I simply call attention to the obvious, viz., that *so far as these arguments are concerned,* the orderer and creator might be completely omni*malevolent* as well, for the arguments give no hint whatever as to his character.

On the other hand, the Ontological and Moral Arguments definitely do conclude an omnibenevolent deity. However, the logical forms employed by each will support the existence of anti-God as effectively as God when premises of each argument are replaced by others that are equally acceptable. David and Majorie Haight illustrate this feature for the Ontological Argument.[5] They distinguish "being great" in a good sense from "being great" in a bad sense, and then the two arguments stand as follows:

---

[4] "Natural Theology: Theism or AntiTheism?" *Sophia* Vol 36(1), (March-April 1997): 75-83.
[5] David and Majorie Haight, "An Ontological Argument for the Devil," *The Monist,* Vol. 54 (1970): 218-220.

From Faith to Doubt…and Life as a Failed Believer

Anselm's Original Argument

1. God is that than which nothing greater (in the good sense) can be conceived.
2. An existing God is greater (in the good sense) than an imaginary God.
3. Therefore, God exists.

The Haights' Parallel Argument (using my term)

1. Anti-God is that than which nothing greater (in the bad sense) can be conceived.
2. An existing anti-God is greater (in the bad sense) than an imaginary one.
3. Therefore, anti-God exists.

Now God and anti-God can't both exist since there cannot be two omnipotent beings (for then each would be more powerful than the other). And since there seems to be no way to choose between, it seems the two arguments have the effect cancelling each other out.

Now, likewise, I proposed the logic of the Moral Argument provides the same opportunity for a parallel support for anti-God. That is, while a summary of Kant's Moral Argument for God is:

1. Happiness ought to be awarded according to moral goodness.
2. Whatever ought to be is possible.
3. The only way possible for happiness to be awarded according to moral goodness is for God to exist.
4. Therefore, God exists

while a parallel argument for the existence of anti-God could be:

1. Misery ought not to be awarded according to moral goodness.
2. Whatever ought not to be is possible.

3. The only way possible for misery to be awarded according to moral goodness is for anti-God to exist.
4. Therefore, anti-God exists.

So as with the Ontological Argument, the two versions of the Moral Argument seem to cancel each other out. Furthermore, I think similar reverse parallels can be devised for all the other "quasi-popular" arguments listed earlier.

However, a "Problem of Goodness" would present itself for this view since it seems a thoroughly evil creator would not tolerate the blessings so many people enjoy. However, I argued that whatever defense theists give for the Problem of Evil can be advanced in reverse just as successfully for the "anti-theist." For example, if the theist blames the moral evil in the world on human free will, the anti-theist could account for the world's moral goodness by human freewill as well; and if the theist claims that world's natural evil promotes human values that over-compensate for it, the anti-theist can claim that the world's natural goodness serves to promote human evils (jealousy, hatred, despair, etc.) that outweigh it.

So, even if all the other criticisms of a traditional argument for the existence or nonexistence of God were successfully met, I think I would still find this anti-God criticism sufficient to leave me in question about it. Of course, not everyone would agree. For example, a preeminent Australian philosopher[6] responded to it in a later issue of the same journal, and I'm sure many Christians would agree with

---

[6] Peter Forrest, "God, Anti-God and the Emotions: A Response to Murphree," *Sophia* Vol 37(1) (March-April 1998): 154-159. (Also see my "God and Anti-God: A Reply to Forrest," *Sophia* Vol 39(1), (March-April 2000): 231-246.

From Faith to Doubt...and Life as a Failed Believer

his claim. He proposes that some people truly know that God exists; accordingly, he concludes that even though the traditional arguments may not select God over anti-God, that there must nevertheless be a special source of knowledge that does.

Also, I suppose many would agree with Tal's objection in personal correspondence with me—: he contends *anti-God* is not a coherent concept to begin with. Rather, he claims that evil is a deviation from good in the same way that, for example, *uncircular* is a deviation from *circular*. So, just as it makes sense to call something absolutely circular it also makes sense to call God absolutely good; however, just as it makes no sense to call something absolutely (or completely, or maximally) uncircular, it makes no sense to call anything absolutely (or completely, or maximally) evil, as I have defined anti-God.

Chapter 5 Looking Back

Once I had decided to question seriously whether God exists, I don't see how I could have avoided the agnostic position to which I arrived. Indeed, I have often wondered whether I was just an "agnostic waiting to happen" from the start; if not, I wonder how much, if any, of my decision to question was a matter of my free will, and how much was a result of my unique life-experiences. For example, I wonder if I ever would have seriously questioned

if I hadn't had that third grade assignment about the Eskimo boy, or

if the restrictions of my home-taught religion had not made me feel ostracized at school, or

if I hadn't yielded to the temptation to smoke that lone cigarette I found, or

if the mission girl had not asked if I knew for sure that Christianity was true.

I guess I just wonder if I ever came close to being the citizen of Christianity for which I was baptized as an infant, and to which I committed my future in my youth. And, out of curiosity, I wonder why Sarah and Tal never questioned as seriously as I.

Perhaps Sarah would claim she did. At least, she relates that as a college freshman she questioned in earnest. Her approach was to wonder what she would, or should, believe if all her religious role models renounced Christianity. So, for a full semester she supposed that our parents, our beloved church pastors, the Camp Meeting evangelists, the young Billy Graham, and so on and on, all concurred that Christianity was a historical fraud. Where would that leave her and her faith?

From Faith to Doubt...and Life as a Failed Believer

Her conclusion was that although this would be most unsettling, she would still believe because of the powerful ethics that Jesus taught—the ethics of helping the poor and needy; etc. Of course, the inference that Christianity is true because the ethics Jesus taught is powerful is not valid unless additional assumptions are made. But perhaps she made them; at least the reasoning was sufficient to sustain, and perhaps even to strengthen, her Christian life. In fact, she and her husband, Ken, are missionaries, and have made "helping the poor and needy in the name of Jesus" their whole lives' work.[7]

So, I think many Christians would say that sincere questioning—if done in the right spirit—is not only allowable, but can even help expose the authenticity of Christianity. Accordingly, I have wondered whether my inquiry was as innocent as my sister's since it served to undermine, rather than to strengthen, my faith, and more than a few Christian friends who knew us both concluded that it could not have been.

Indeed, I think Christians hold universally that it is impossible to begin doubting God's existence while walking with him. Rather, in order for such doubt to become possible one first has to be separated from him by some intervening sin. And Christian friends have questioned me, and speculated as to the nature of the sin that precipitated my skepticism.

(i) One suggestion proposed that my inquiry was contaminated from the start by a deep dissatisfaction with Christianity, and that this explained why my questioning led to skepticism while Sarah's led to a deeper faith.

---

[7] See the website of the missionary organization they founded at www.sifat.org.

That is, those who knew me knew I had been attracted by worldly pleasure and was not happy that those who enjoyed it were to suffer in hell. So, the reasoning went that my sister's motive for questioning was pure, for she merely wanted to confirm the truth that we had both been taught, but my motive for questioning was dishonest, for I was secretly looking for an excuse to reject that truth. Accordingly, I used the mission girl's crisis as an opportunity to launch an inquiry which I secretly hoped would end in doubt, and my skeptical conclusion was simply the fulfillment of that deep-seated, sinful desire which directed the course of my inquiry. Moreover, if the convenient opportunity of the mission girl's crisis had not arisen, the speculation was that I would have found some other pretext to justify the very same undertaking.

However, so far as I know myself, this is simply not true. Of course, the motive might not have been simple or singular and, by the nature of the case, I can't say what any subconscious drives might have been. Also, through the years I suppose my repeated inquires could have been prompted by a variety of motives, but I strongly believe that the desire to escape Christianity was never among them. Rather, then, as now, *if the punishment of hell awaits a life of worldliness, I wanted to know about it!*

But, whatever the case, the more important point is that integrity of an inquiry need not be compromised by the motive that instigates it. For if it were, the Christians who would dismiss my inquiry on the basis of its alleged motive would also have to dismiss Sarah's inquiry on the same ground—as merely being the directed fulfillment of her antecedent desire to confirm Christianity.

(ii) Another interesting charge of dishonesty proposed that I handled the result of my inquiry unfairly. It proposed that since I found the arguments for and against the existence of God inconclusive both ways that the existing strength of my belief should not have been affected either way, and that I should have retained the same degree of faith I possessed when I undertook the inquiry. But, instead, I

From Faith to Doubt...and Life as a Failed Believer

allowed my failure to find *additional* support for theism to steal away the measure of faith I already had. And this, claimed some of my Christian friends, was cheating.

But in response I must say that it was not the mere absence of additional support for Christianity that caused my faith to fail but, rather, *the absence of additional support when I had been led to believe there was additional support.* In fact, ever since I rested in the belief that my educated parents would have known it if Christianity had been false, I always supposed that there was this balance of evidence or level of understanding that justified the belief. Moreover, this picture was continually reinforced as I matured, as the adults in my world apparently all thought it was foolish to doubt, and all my pastors and learned professors avowed that adequate support for Christianity was there and available to anyone who seriously searched for it. I had always taken their word for this, so when the mission girl asked if *I really knew* Christianity was true I felt I must internalize this verification for myself in order to answer her properly. But then, when I searched for myself and failed to find it, it made the position feel groundless and I was left not knowing what to believe.

So, it is not as if my search yielded nothing new; rather, it exposed that the overwhelming evidence I thought the saints bore witness to was not within my reach at all; or, at least, it was not there in the way I expected it to be.

Perhaps these saints would have replied—and I think many of them actually did—that they were not talking about objective inquiry where one would investigate disinterestedly and passively wait for some convincing evidence or insight to override one's doubts. Rather, they were speaking of an inner assurance—when "the Spirit itself beareth witness with our spirit" [Rom. 8:16]—that comes upon actively surrendering one's will to God. And this assurance, they would claim, is what is so overwhelming that it shows all philosophical arguments for the existence of God to be useless and trivial by contrast.

Wallace Murphree

In response I can only say that I have never had such assurance, whatever others may have experienced. Of course earlier, when I was a Christian, I did believe that I had it, but now I am convinced I was mistaken. For example, I felt certain at the Camp Meeting altar that day that God forgave my sins (from which it follows that God exists). Indeed, I felt so certain about it I would have staked the eternal welfare of all humanity on its truth at the time. But now I am convinced that what I saw for certain that day was not that "God forgave my sins" at all; rather, what was certain was the validity of the reasoning the evangelist gave. That is, he pointed out (roughly):

> Premise 1: If you confess your sins [etc.] God forgives your sins.
> Premise 2: You confess your sins [etc.].
> Conclusion: Therefore, God forgives your sins.

Now this reasoning is "certain" in that the premises, when taken together, certainly entail the conclusion, for it is impossible for the premises both to be true while the conclusion is false. But that is to say that *what* is certain is the "if-then" sentence below *as a whole,*

> *If both of these premises are true* then the conclusion is true,

rather than either of its clauses separately.

But I mistakenly attached the certainty I felt to the conclusion alone, i.e., to the "then" clause of the sentence, and thought it certain that "God forgives my sin." Of course, I believed both premises at the time, so it was rational for me to believe the conclusion as well. But by the same token, since I now doubt Premise 1 (because I doubt that there is a God), the argument no longer provides reason to believe that the conclusion is true—even though that conclusion does follow *for certain* from the two premises.

I think the same considerations hold, *mutatis mutandis*, for each of the many other experiences of assurance I had in my Christian life. For example, I had a deep feeling of assurance when I sensed of the return

From Faith to Doubt...and Life as a Failed Believer

of Jesus' presence that beautiful evening in the woods after I returned from the army. However, that assurance was based on, and was no stronger than, my antecedent belief that the God of Christianity exists. Again, at the time I believed it with all my heart, and so the assurance naturally seemed absolute; but as the belief in God's existence weakened, the assurance that it was Jesus' presence I felt—rather than some wish-fulfilling illusion—faded as well.

And in so far as I can ascertain, I have never been provided any reason to believe in God's existence from my religious experiences, because my belief in God's existence always preceded, and was a necessary condition for, those very experiences.

That is, in the same way that my pre-school belief in the existence of Satan did not emerge from my temptations to disobey my parents, my belief in the existence of God did not emerge from my feeling of forgiveness or holiness. Rather, in both cases alike, I simply interpreted the experiences as they occurred in terms of the belief-categories that I already possessed. And, while I can't presume to know what the religious experiences of others may be, I can't help but suspect that my case may be typical. For example, if two people have an identical dream about God, the believer might honestly report that

God spoke to me in a dream,

while the skeptic would say

I dreamed God spoke to me.

But which is correct is not given *in* the dream, and their different reports simply reflect the difference of their antecedent beliefs.

(iii) Finally, accepting that I see no balance of evidence for God's existence, Christian friends have often demurred that there are many other things I accept on faith when I have no balance of evidence to support them, and so if I were really honest I would suspend my belief in them as well. Otherwise, they claim, I have no justification for suspending my Christian beliefs.

I do acknowledge that I have no balance of evidence to support many of my other beliefs. Indeed, perhaps most my everyday beliefs are of this sort. For example, I drive the car without evidence that the steering and brakes will work again today, and retire to bed without evidence that the house will hold up for yet another night. Etc. However, even without having the evidence myself, I believe there exists evidence that would support my beliefs in these cases and that I could have it if I investigated—and this is exactly how I felt about, and how I easily accepted, Christianity for so long.

Moreover, if after investigating the car or the house I did not find the expected evidence that it was still dependable I would lose whatever earlier faith I had to the contrary; and this is exactly what happened when I failed to find the support for Christianity that I expected. So, I don't see an inconsistency with the way I handle these two sets of beliefs.

But in addition to these practical cases, I also acknowledge that I believe one side, rather than the other, on many theoretical issues in the absence of favorable support. For example, (although it may seem a little surprising when one first thinks about it) there seems to be no evidence at all, and hence no of balance of evidence, supporting either answer to any of the following questions:

1. Is there such a thing as truth?
2. Is knowledge possible?
3. Do there exist any persons other than myself? (Perhaps all the others are just cleverly disguised robots.)
4. Did the past really occur? (Maybe everything—including ourselves with fully stocked memories, libraries full of history books, rocks full of fossils, etc., all first popped into existence ten seconds ago.)
5. Etc.

From Faith to Doubt...and Life as a Failed Believer

Yet, even without justifying evidence I strongly believe the affirmative position on each of these. Indeed, here I don't know how *not* to believe these things, even though I admit I have no balance of evidence for them. Rather, I simply find these "basic beliefs" irresistible—and I suppose others may find the belief in the existence of God to be of this sort as well. However, I find both the belief that "God exists" and the belief that "God does not exist" equally contestable, and so I simply do not how to believe one over the other—like I don't know how to believe the coin will land on heads rather than tails. Of course, I could "call it" one way or the other, but that is not the same.

So, here I am not claiming that my skepticism is rationally justified, although I think it is. But my point, rather, is to report the personal fact that I no longer knew how to believe that God exists once I became convinced that it has no greater rational support than its opposing view.

So in spite of charges to the contrary, I feel sure that I arrived at skepticism honestly or, if anything, I actually gave theism the benefit of the doubt as I inquired. For one reason, I was reluctant to turn loose of my belief for fear that there might be a God who would send unbelievers to hell; for another, I knew my defection would cause some who loved me great consternation—which it did.

(iv) But if my skepticism was not the result of dishonesty, then Christian friends contended it must have been precipitated by some other wrongdoing. And those who had earlier heard me testify to the knowledge of God's saving grace, but then later heard me claim it never happened, reasonably supposed that I had strayed into worldly sin of some sort that separated me from the assurance that once was mine. That is, they concluded that I had been saved and that I knew it with certainty, but that with my intervening sins God allowed me to forget it.

Wallace Murphree

In fact, Daddy proposed my skepticism might be a product of my smoking, for I agreed with him that smoking was wrong. And I think I can see how this analysis made sense to him; in fact, if I—as a young Christian—could have foreseen my later skepticism, I think I would have considered this a reasonable account for it as well. However, even should it be true, it cannot be credible to me as a skeptic, since one would already have to believe that God exists in order to see the theory as a possibility.

***

So, I am convinced my skepticism was neither a product of dishonesty nor of yielding to the temptations of worldly sin. However, I did often feel guilty as I was questioning, especially in the beginning, and I think this was because of my conception of the role of belief in Christianity. Specifically, not only did I think belief was a prerequisite for salvation, but I also thought of it as a duty—: that is, I thought it was a duty to believe that God exists, that the Bible is true, etc., just like it was a duty not to lie, steal, and kill.

In fact, I thought this was what every Christian child grew up believing. However, I learned later that Tal never thought of it so when he was young. Rather, he just grew up believing that God really exists, perhaps like we both grew up believing that there is such a thing as truth; or, maybe it was more like how we both grew up believing that our parents loved us—: we just believed without the shadow of a doubt. And, it well may be that his Christian youth was more typical than mine in that respect. In fact, it seems to me that this was Martha's orientation as well. At any rate, Christianity, as I understood it, commanded me to keep the faith, and it was then to provide the basis for every other facet of my life.

So as I see it now, my ultimate sin, i.e., my "sin of no return," indeed, my "unpardonable sin," was my *decision to seek a rational foundation for my faith* after I was unable to answer the girl at the mission the way I thought she deserved to be answered. I knew better; indeed, the injunction I had often quoted to others was, "Trust in the

From Faith to Doubt...and Life as a Failed Believer

Lord with all thine heart; and lean not unto thine own understanding." [Proverbs 3:5]

But that's not what I did; rather, I tried to anchor my faith in reason (my understanding). And *that* was the sin—to adopt reason as a more ultimate touchstone than faith. This was not a sin of dishonesty, or of forbidden pleasure; but it was a sin of disobedience. Of course, today I don't think of it as a sin against God; but it was a sin against my religion which at the time I believed to channel the commands of God.

I knew what my religion would have had me do instead—: I should have prayed, and prayed; and I should not have left my knees until I "had the victory." Of course, I did pray some; daily, for months at least, I prayed the New Testament prayer, "Lord, I believe; help thou my unbelief" all through the days. But that's not what my religion commanded. I should have determined to pray—to "fast and pray"— until my doubts had subsided and I "knew within myself" the truth to tell the mission girl. Of course, now I believe I never could have known, even if I had prayed until I died. But my sin consisted of the fact that I didn't even try with that type of earnestness.

So, (to dramatize it, because it's how I often feel about it), I took what my parents believed my most precious inheritance, the faith they strived so diligently to nourish and protect for me, and entered it, as it were, into competition with unbelief. And while I insist that the contest was fair and impartial, I can't maintain my innocence, for I "sinned" by allowing the competition to begin with. So this confirms the Christian claim that some intervening sin separated me from my faith, for it shows how I became a traitor before I became a skeptic— and how my skepticism was a result of that treason.

But although I admit I sinned against my religion, I have come to believe that my religion also sinned against me—and many, many others—and continues to do so today. So, in spite of all the good it has done and is doing, I have become angry at it in a way I never could have expected.

But I'm not angry at Christians, not even at those who seem never to tire in their evangelistic zeal; for, so far as I know, they are among the best people on earth. And, too, it really doesn't make much sense to personify and be angry at the religion. However, now I feel that the version of Christianity I once believed in "kidnaps" children into its service, and leaves them no way of escape except "to sin their way free."

I shall describe what seems to be the dynamics of this scheme in the next chapter.

Chapter 6 Is Christianity Evil? A Question of Honesty

The divisions within Christianity are many and there is no consensus as to its exact boundaries; however, for the purposes of this chapter I think it will be fair to consider its definitive beliefs to be those given in the Apostles' Creed, as follows:

> I believe in God the Father Almighty,
> maker of heaven and earth;
>
> And in Jesus Christ his only Son our Lord:
> who was conceived by the Holy Spirit,
> born of the Virgin Mary,
> suffered under Pontius Pilate,
> was crucified, dead, and buried;*
> the third day he rose from the dead;
> he ascended into heaven,
> and sitteth at the right hand of God the Father Almighty;
> from thence he shall come to judge the quick and the dead.
>
> I believe in the Holy Spirit,
> the holy catholic church,
> the communion of saints,
> the forgiveness of sins,
> the resurrection of the body, and the life everlasting. Amen.[8]

---

[8] *The United Methodist Hymnal,* (Nashville TN: The United Methodist Publishing House, 1998), 881.

*Traditional use of this creed includes these words: "He descended into hell."

But although every Christian holds these beliefs, no believer's complete Christian faith is limited to just these articles. Essential to most perspectives is the additional, extra-Creedal contention that the Bible is the word of God. There are, of course, numerous interpretations of the Bible, but a prevalent overall reading, and the one I grew up with, yields something like the following world picture:

> Out of his goodness, God created heaven and the physical world so that angels and human beings could share the wonder of existence with him. But some of the angels rebelled and led the human race to follow (The Fall), and so justice required that God create hell for them. But out of his mercy for human beings, he—in the person of Jesus—came to earth and was crucified (and went to hell] to satisfy the penalty that justice required. Then, with the debt for their sins thus paid, all human beings have to do to accept forgiveness and reclaim (something like) God's original goal for them is to believe and repent. And the judgment of "…the quick and the dead" will be the final determination of who did and who did not accept that forgiveness. However, it will turn out that most human beings will continue to follow Satan (the chief rebellious angel), and will therefore be found unforgiven on Judgment Day. Consequently, they will suffer eternal hell even though their redemption—tragically unclaimed—had been fully secured by Jesus' sacrifice.

Accordingly, it is infinitely in one's best interest to accept this salvation. Moreover, it is each person's ultimate duty to accept it and, in addition, to lead as many others as possible to do so as well. That is, leading others to salvation is not only the morally decent thing to do but, according to many Christians, the Bible commands it directly when the risen Christ issued the so-called Great Commission to the eleven remaining disciples:

From Faith to Doubt…and Life as a Failed Believer

> Go ye into all the world, and preach the gospel to every creature. He that believeth and is baptized shall be saved; but he that believeth not shall be damned. [Mark 16:15-16]

The common interpretation, including the one I was taught, considers this command to extend to all Christians of all ages, and this curse to nonbelievers universally (although there was some question as to how God would deal with those who had never heard the Christian message).

So, the Christianity of my youth presented itself as God's project of saving as much of fallen humanity as he could. The whole purpose of life on earth, then, was portrayed as the opportunity to accept forgiveness, and the duty to lead as many others as possible to do so as well. Accordingly, nothing else finally matters in the here and now.

On the one hand, this world picture is very simple; in fact, from childhood I grew up believing it. On the other hand, it is so all encompassing that it furnishes the backdrop for every more specialized study; indeed, theology and science, with all their sub-disciplines, are simply matters of filling in the details of this general picture. Consequently, any theology that doesn't conform is heresy, and any scientific theory that doesn't fit is false *ipso facto*.

Such was the self-image of the Christianity I knew. It was not a theory or philosophy that might be studied objectively alongside competing views; instead, it was simply the truth about reality and our place in it. Indeed, it was the Highest Truth—so high that it transcends human reason and is only accessible by faith; and it was the Truth that offers the only possible escape for the individuals of a race otherwise destined for damnation.

Often citing passages from St. Paul, the adults of my teenage milieu would warn young Christians that people of "the world" do not accept this Truth. Indeed, they would remind us that that nature is fallen and depraved, and those of the world are so deceived in their depravity

Wallace Murphree

that the Truth even looks foolish to it. Furthermore, we young Christians were forewarned that if we ever tried to inspect Christianity "objectively" it might come to look foolish to us, too. We were cautioned that one of Satan's wiles is to convince believers that honesty requires their faith to be evaluated by reason and evidence; however, it was explained that what honesty actually requires is that beliefs about *the natural world* be so evaluated, but that the supernatural Truth lies in the transcendent province of faith. So, when Satan would have Christians confuse the two and submit the *supernatural* Truth to the test of *natural* reason, he is simply trying to pry them loose from the saving faith on which their eternal beatitude depends.

This picture held a great deal of power over me but, flouting all warning, I did step back and tried to look at both sides. That is, I questioned whether Christianity is *the* one important Truth about reality or whether it is a very foolish view of things and, as I have reported, I did not found the answer. But although I did not find the answer, in the search the Christianity I had been an advocate of took on a completely different appearance to me—: it appeared to condone, if not actually to promote, dishonesty.

That is, first, when I did step back and tried to look at all sides impartially, there seemed to be as much reason to suspect Christianity of being the agent of falsehood as there was to suspect Satan, the world, or contrary religions. In fact, from this vantage point, the claim that the exalted status of Christian Truth places it beyond human interrogation fails to carry any weight at all since any religion could make the same claim—and any deceptive religion would make it. Indeed, I realized I would have found this deceptive account of Christianity quite sufficient if I had been reared an atheist or an adherent of a different religion.

Furthermore, since deception (stealth, camouflage, etc.) is so effective in the struggle for biological survival, it seemed it might also be effective in the natural selection of religions—if religions are in fact

From Faith to Doubt...and Life as a Failed Believer

natural phenomena. Indeed, this is what I had been taught about "false religions" all along—: their followers had been deceived. And I realized those reared in non-Christian religions likewise thought that Christianity thrived by its great power to deceive the masses. So "from the outside," the honesty of Christianity seemed just as suspect as the honesty of any other view.

Of course, "from the inside" I could never have allowed myself the thought that Christianity might propagate itself dishonestly, for it would have been blasphemy even to consider it seriously; but, when attempting to look at the matter impartially, the suspicion seemed as natural for it as for any other religion. Then, once I was free to suspect it, it became progressively more apparent that one version of Christianity—the version of my childhood—is indeed steeped in dishonesty.

But this is not a gross dishonesty, like a conspiracy of hypocrites who deliberately deceive the people. Rather, my claim is that while overtly commanding honesty, the teachings of the religion insidiously encourage dishonest belief, and insidiously encourage its followers to become complicit in the promotion of dishonest belief in others. Then, in turn, the community of believers enthusiastically welcomes the dishonest converts into its fold.

The two teachings that I find specifically conducive to Christian dishonesty, already mentioned above, are that

> it is in one's self-interest to believe Christianity, and that
> it is one's duty never to abandon this belief.

I shall refer to this version of the religion as "Belief-premium Christianity" and later contrast it with what I call "Love-premium Christianity." My accusation simply is that Belief-premium Christianity naturally encourages dishonesty in a way that Love-premium Christianity does not. For I propose:

Wallace Murphree

Whenever belief is the prize, honesty stands to be a stumbling block; and whenever belief is a duty, honesty stands to be a sin.

Belief-premium Christianity

(1) Self-interest

Belief-premium Christianity preaches it is in one's highest self-interest to believe and those not firmly established in atheism or some other religion often feel this contention merits serious consideration, as do most Christians when they are tempted to defect.

Although my parents didn't emphasize the self-interest aspect of Christianity, the doctrine of the benefit of belief and the detriment of doubt certainly weighed heavily on my thoughts when I first began to question. Moreover, I have heard many others admit its overwhelming influence on their decisions. In fact, quite a few students through the years have volunteered that they had occasionally wondered whether God really exists (or whether Christianity is really true), but felt it would be taking too big a chance with their eternal well-being to explore the question seriously. Furthermore, married couples have told me that they, themselves, had been skeptics, but felt they had no right to put their children at such risk. So, when they became parents they re-entered the church community in order to rear their sons and daughters in whatever safety the religion might provide.

Pascal's Wager

Although people may have been drawn by such considerations from the early times, Blaise Pascal [1623-1662] provided a catchy self-interest argument for accepting Christianity that has since become standard. In "The Wager," he pictures our time on earth as a gaming

From Faith to Doubt...and Life as a Failed Believer

place where each of us must bet our lives on whether God exists. As far as we can tell the odds are even since the arguments for and against God's existence are equally compelling. Still, we have to place our bets and, since the odds are even, the one consideration left—and the one that then should rationally determine our decision—is the payoff. Now the *God exists* bet pays eternal life if it turns out to be the winner (i.e., if it is true), but it pays nothing whatever if it is not, while the *God does not exist* bet pays nothing whatever if it turns out to be the winner, but it pays out a sentence of eternal damnation if it is not.

So, there is everything to gain and nothing to lose by betting one's life on *God exists,* while one has everything to lose and nothing to gain by betting his or her life on *God does not exist.* Accordingly, Pascal claims that even though reason and evidence are *theoretically* inconclusive, there is still every *practical* justification for believing that God exists. That is, his way of thinking doesn't provide rational support for the truth of theism but, instead, it offers a self-interest motive for accepting it whether it is true or not.

Surely Pascal's recommendation would be prudent if one were considering how to bet in an actual casino or, perhaps, vote in an actual election; but since people do not have the same (easy) control over their beliefs that they have over their money or ballots, this may seem like an exceptionally difficult—if not an impossible—recommendation that Pascal proposes. The problem is that skeptics must convince themselves that God really does exist in order to make the *God exists* bet, and this is like having to convince oneself that the coin will actually land on heads while believing the odds are just as great that it will land on tails.

Of course, Pascal is aware of this quandary; but rather than having skeptics reconsider the traditional arguments in a more favorable light, he recommends instead that they come to the faith naturally, as little children who are reared in religion do. Specifically, he recommends that they put themselves in a position to be convinced by

69

becoming part of a community of believers and by acting as if they also believed: they should "attend masses", "take holy waters," etc. Then this, Pascal holds, will naturally cure the uncertainty in due time, and the risk-free bet will have been successfully placed.

Today this strategy might be called an instance of the "fake it 'til you make it" technique, which is touted as an effective behavioral therapy. But the strategy, itself, is morally neutral, and can be employed in the service of honesty or of dishonesty. For example, it is used to promote a truthful and realistic outlook when it helps one overcome an irrational fear or brings one's faltering self-confidence up to his or her true level of competence. But Pascal would employ it to perform the reverse operation. That is, rather than using it to transform one's unfounded self-doubt into a well-founded self-confidence, he would employ it transform the skeptic's well-founded religious doubt into an unfounded religious belief. That is, in Pascal's hands it becomes an instrument of self-deception.

Of course, we may honestly choose *to act* as if one possibility is true—as when we bet on heads rather than tails, or vote for one candidate rather than the other. But this is completely different from attempting to overcome honest doubt by deliberately putting ourselves in a setting that systematically brushes all evidence and reason for the doubt aside, as Pascal would have skeptics do. In fact, as far as honesty is concerned, I think this Pascalian move is the moral the equivalent of hiring a hypnotist or taking a credulity drug in order to establish the desired the belief.

Moreover, while skeptical adults are advised to seek out Christian activities for themselves, they are urged to provide these for their children from the start by rearing them in a religious environment; and belief-premium parents naturally make every effort to do this. They provide a Christian home for them, saturate them in church activities, send them to religious schools, and attempt to shield them from anything that might thwart the development of their faith. Moreover, these parents tell their children that God has given them

From Faith to Doubt...and Life as a Failed Believer

assurance of his existence and that he answers their prayers and miraculously protects them through all the days of their lives; and, furthermore, they claim it is this view of life that will then secure a safe and joyous afterlife.

So with this rearing, the children cannot be expected to be impartial jurors when the question of the truth of these beliefs has to be confronted. But, of course, this is the whole purpose of the Christian upbringing—: to prejudice children in favor of Christianity so as "not to give the devil a fair chance."

When I was a Christian it didn't occur to me that attempting to believe out of self-interest, and encouraging others to do so, might be dishonest; nor did I think of it as being especially widespread. However now, as I do consider it to be dishonest, I also find it to be very extensive. But I would not be surprised if many current Christians think my estimation of its scope to be exaggerated.

But why I feel such dishonesty to be so pervasive can be seen by the following "thought experiment," and I also believe it might help others become aware of its extent. The experiment simply asks that we suppose it to be in our best interest for our beliefs to be correct and that to be mistaken will have dire consequences.

Specifically, rather than supposing with Pascal that

> *It is in our best interest to believe that God exists (whether it is true or not),*

let us suppose instead that

> *It is in our best interest to believe the truth (whether it is "God exists" or not).*

Now, while today's believers include all those who might believe out of self-interest, no one would believe from self-interest on the new

Wallace Murphree

supposition for it would simply not be in anyone's self-interest to do so. Accordingly, the difference between the present number of believers and the number there would be on this new supposition should serve as an index as to how extensive the dishonesty based on self-interest actually is.

The "Grand Metaphysical Exam"

Instead of casting this second supposition as a casino bet, I shall pose it as a one-question, true/false "Grand Metaphysical Exam" that everyone is required to read, sign, and turn in. It might look like the one below.

The significant difference between the Wager and the Exam is that the latter allows for skepticism by not forcing an answer, whereas the former does not. In fact, "forcing the bet" is what gives the Wager its compelling edge, and Belief-premium Christians would surely find the Exam religiously irrelevant since it fails to reflect this forced character of belief-premium religion.

But the Exam is not really designed to be religiously relevant; rather, it is designed to test the scope of faith-based dishonesty, and for this purpose it is essential to have a place for agnostics.

So, let us suppose everyone agrees the Exam is valid and takes it, signs it, and turns it in. And then let us ask how the post-test Christian, atheist, and agnostic populations would then differ from the pretest populations.

First, I suggest that both the Christian and atheist populations would likely show some percentage reduction as those who had casually inherited their view are now forced to consider the question seriously. That is, I suppose a percentage of both of these erstwhile populations would, now on second thought, register as agnostics by turning their copies of the Exam in unmarked.

From Faith to Doubt...and Life as a Failed Believer

ONE-QUESTION
GRAND METAPHYSICAL EXAM

Instructions: Indicate your answer by checking 1 or 2; *if you are not sure and choose not to guess, you may sign the test paper and turn it in unmarked.*

Explanation of Results: Those who mark the correct answer will be awarded eternal happiness, while those who mark the incorrect answer will be condemned to eternal torment; *and those who turn their papers in unmarked will receive no reward or penalty whatever.*

****

God exists.
1. ( )True
2. ( )False

Signature_____

But while I doubt that there would be a further reduction in atheism, I think the tally would show a drastic *additional* exodus from the professing Christian camp into agnosticism; and this additional number would be those of a Pascalian persuasion who had not yet

Wallace Murphree

"made it" to a firm belief and—now faced with the prospect of eternal torment—are forced to admit that they were "faking it."

Moreover, if the Exam were re-administered for successive generation it would continually arrest those in the process of "faking it," so that the pool of those who had "made it" as dishonest believers would not be repopulated. Furthermore, conscientious parents would now warn their children about the perils of holding a false belief on the issue, religious experiences would be analyzed critically, fantastic testimonies would be received with suspicion, public support for Christian institutions would dwindle, etc., etc., until finally there would be no Pascalian believers remaining.

Now, as this stage is finally reached in our thought experiment, we can compare our supposed present-day Christian population with what we expect its remaining population would be. And if we believe the reduction would be great then, by the same token, we believe that dishonesty based on self-interest is correspondingly widespread in present-day Christianity. As I said above, I believe it would be very great. Indeed, I think dishonesty so motivated is pandemic in Christianity today.

Self-interest and Dishonesty

But even acknowledging that Pascal's recommendation is inherently dishonest, there remains the question as to whether it should not be advocated even in spite of that.

I mentioned earlier that this was an important consideration for me as I began doubting, and I'm sure it forestalled my full-fledged questioning for some time at least. And even today I must admit that that if I thought holding certain beliefs stood to make the difference between eternal bliss and everlasting torment I would—in all prudent cowardice—try with all my might to acquire them.

From Faith to Doubt...and Life as a Failed Believer

Furthermore, I think it would be ultimately fastidious to advocate what stood to be a hell-condemning honesty over what might be a soul-saving affectation for others. So, if I thought holding certain beliefs made this type of difference, I would do absolutely everything within my power to ensure my children held them. I would say "honesty be damned," and employ whatever methods of indoctrination I thought most efficient. And if ordinary religious instruction seemed too slow or unsure, I would explore the possibility of hypnosis—and hope that medical science could soon produce a pill that would dispose children to believe, or perhaps discover some sort of vaccine against religious doubt. And it seems to me that any loving parent would do the same.

So, given the view that belief in God is vital to a child's eternal welfare, I certainly would not fault parents who would avail themselves of *any* technique that would insure it; and I would not fault any educator or public official for recommending it. In fact, I would fault them if they did not. And by the same token, I certainly cannot fault contemporary preachers, teachers, or other proselytizers who, in want of a vaccination, try to dispel the doubt any way that they can—however extreme it might seem to others.

Accordingly, under his analysis of the circumstances I cannot condemn Pascal for advocating "fake it 'til you make it"; indeed, I would think him a monster if his mantra had been "honesty whatever the cost." Furthermore, I really don't find the logic of his analysis to be faulty, assuming—as the Wager does—that there are no viable non-Christian religions.

But I do find his recommendation unsound because, even if one could make it by faking it, I cannot believe a good God would approve of it. At least this is how it has seemed to me every time I have imagined standing in God's judgment.

From early childhood I have often tried to picture Judgment Day as realistically as I could. At first, of course, I was trying to preview a possibly terrifying event that I thought was sure to be in my future; but even after I began to have doubts I continued to imagine it hypothetically from time to time. And each time I considered it, I found I had far rather face God having been an honest skeptic than a contrived believer. *Indeed, the prospects of standing in the presence of God* **as a phoney** *is still about as terrifying as anything I can imagine.*

So I have never been able picture God's approval of a Pascalian belief in his existence. Instead, it always seemed clear that God would simply judge such a belief to be what it is; and what it is, to put it in blunt terms, is the theft of a commodity the skeptic thinks could be to his or her eternal advantage. It is a *theft* because the Pascalian believer has no honest right to it.

In addition, I cannot imagine that it would please God for his creatures to claim he has spoken to them—or that he has revealed himself to them, or that he has given them proof of his existence, or that he has answered their prayer, etc.,—if he hasn't. And, it well may bring him special displeasure if they have convinced themselves of these things in a protracted attempt to appease and outwit him and thereby scheme their way into his higher favor.

Accordingly, if God does exist, I think there is nothing we could possibly gain by a Pascalian faith. We might deceive ourselves or our children; but since one cannot deceive God we would thereby simply put ourselves in the position to suffer whatever penalty the self-deception might justly incur.

(2) Duty

Most people hold that self-interest is not our only motive but that that we are motivated by a sense of duty as well. One's conscience is the faculty thought to perceive duty and Christians often claim that it "is the voice of the Holy Spirit."

From Faith to Doubt…and Life as a Failed Believer

So in addition to the Pascalian motive of self-interest, Belief-premium Christians who may be tempted to doubt are also motivated to keep the faith out of a sense of duty. Indeed, as was mentioned earlier, many contend that losing the faith is the unpardonable sin, so the duty to believe would oppose any inclination to question it.

Accordingly, young Christians are typically forewarned that they may be tempted to doubt, but instructed that they must remain steadfast in the faith. Also, they are cautioned that their own intellects will be powerless against Satan's devious guile and that, therefore, their only recourse is to call on God's power in prayer, scripture reading, etc., whenever this occurs. So, in general, when children receive such Christian education, the "good ones" consistently do their duty and resist each temptation to doubt; and they thereby grow and mature in the faith, and preserve the religion for the next generation. And by their own standards, they are absolutely right to do this, because their only other option risks the sin of unbelief.

Elsewhere[9] I have called such religious training "intellectual kidnapping," and claimed it to be "good-child abuse." That is, it is "*good*-child" abuse since only those escape who, such as I, would "sin their way free." But good children, like many of my young Christian friends, will not do that. So I think it is obvious that dishonesty thrives as these good children conscientiously squelch their inclinations to doubt and grow into fine Christian men and women.

---

[9] "On Evangelizing Children: Breaking the Cycle of Dogmatic Belief Systems," in *Marginal Groups and Mainstream American Culture,* ed. Yolanda Estes, *et al.* (Lawrence KS: University Press of Kansas, 2000), 172-92,

Wallace Murphree

However, the duty is not merely a deterrent keeping those tempted to doubt in line, but it also stands as an ideal that captures the noble aspirations of youth reared in the faith. That is, as children are instructed in the belief-premium view, they are taught it is their duty to live and breathe it, to marry someone of the faith, and to rear their children—and to rear their children to rear their children—in its truth. Then for their part, the children make total and life-long commitments to it as they first accept its promised saving grace and, so committed, the life of loyalty stands as the highest ideal and the loss of faith as the paradigm of treachery.

In fact, among the sincerest memories of my youth is the hallowed feeling I would have in church or Camp Meeting as everyone joined together and sang:

> Faith of our fathers, holy faith,
> We will be true to thee 'til death.[10]

That was my commitment then and, to the extent that I knew myself, the matter was settled, for I was resolved to remain true forever. Furthermore, my young Christian friends all made the same commitment.

Duty and Dishonesty

But even admitting belief based on duty is essentially dishonest, there remains the question as to whether it might still be rightfully advocated even in spite of that.

---

[10] Frederick W. Faber

From Faith to Doubt...and Life as a Failed Believer

Certainly Christians generally accept honesty as a duty, and it is universally held that, in themselves, duties are all compatible with each other. However, it is also generally recognized that the *application* of duties in real situations often do conflict. For example, it is a duty to tell the truth, and it is a duty to prevent murder whenever it is possible; and, although these duties are inherently compatible with each other, a situation could arise in which the only way to prevent the murder is by telling a lie. In such cases the standard doctrine is that one should follow the duty that conscience discerns to have the higher priority; that is when both duties cannot be performed, one should perform the "stronger" of the two, and performing the weaker of the two instead would then be sin.

So, for Belief-premium Christians the duty to believe trumps every other duty if there is a conflict, for "without faith it is impossible to please [God]." [Hebrews 11:6] Accordingly, if one has a conflict between keeping the faith and being honest, being honest would be the sin.

Moreover, for one who might question this priority, the standard reply is:

> Nay but, O man, who art thou that repliest against God? [Romans 9:20]

As a struggling Christian I always found this rhetorical question from Romans very intimidating. But now as a skeptic I do not see myself as replying *against God* at all; rather, I see myself as replying against what I feel to be unsupported assertions that Christians make. And in this capacity, I am responding in the very same way Christians would respond to analogous claims advanced by adherents of other religions. For example, an exasperated Arab might exclaim,

> Nay but, O American, who art thou that repliest against Allah?

or the Eskimo boy might chide,

> Nay but, O Alabaman, who art thou that repliest against The Old Woman who lives under the sea?

But Christians would rightly respond, "We are not replying *against* Allah or The Old Woman; rather, we simply question your human claims." And, again, as a skeptic of Christianity I certainly do not see myself as replying *against God* but, rather, as merely questioning the human claims that Christians advance.

And among these I question the claim that a totally good creator would command his creatures to believe he exists without providing evidence or understanding that would make that belief an honest one. Instead, if such an imperative were issued from "on high," I believe it would not be from the good God of Christianity. Rather, such a command would put creatures in the very type of conundrum one might expect anti-God to devise, for then they would be damned if they did believe [sin of dishonesty] and damned if they didn't [sin of unbelief].

Summary: Belief-premium Christianity

So, it certainly seems to me that neither self-interest nor duty overrides the moral demands of honesty on the issue as to whether God exists; in spite of that, however, I think that dishonesty concerning it is a very prevalent condition in Christianity.

As I said earlier, I was not aware of this when I was a Christian; or, perhaps, I just wouldn't allow myself to notice this "elephant at the altar" back then. However, now I suspect it crowds the honest believers to the edges, and I wonder if it hasn't always been this way.

Perhaps I failed to notice it earlier because I didn't see the distinction as being important back then—for *having* the belief, regardless of how it originated and is maintained, was what I thought really mattered at that time.

From Faith to Doubt…and Life as a Failed Believer

Or, perhaps I failed to notice it because I was a dishonest believer, and such dishonesty systematically hides itself. That is, on the one hand, Pascalian believers will not admit their dishonesty while they are "faking it" (for that would defeat the whole project), while those who have successfully "made it" no longer see their beliefs to be faked—just as those who have come to believe their own lies no longer believe them to be lies. And on the other hand, those who refuse to question out of duty typically tell themselves they are resisting deception, rather than resisting honest inquiry.

Again, the dishonesty I suspect is not that of scheming hypocrites, however few or many of these there may be. Rather, I am referring to what I think to be an institutionally condoned behavior that is so prevalent it probably thrives in every Christian community, and perhaps at some time, to some degree, even in most individual believers. And unlike the stereotypical hypocrite who deceives others in order to exploit them, the dishonesty of even the worst of these believers is simply their attempt to plan responsibly for they own long-range destinies. But in addition, the group also includes myriads of the most noble people on earth who are trying their best to discharge their duty and do what they believe will be of highest eternal value but, in order to do so, are forced to sacrifice their honesty on the altar of their faith.

I am indignant about this religion-sanctioned deceit, but I am unable to find a proper target for my wrath. I am convinced that a good God would not have ordained it, but I also believe that the people who perpetrate its spread are conscientiously doing what they believe to be right and good; and since I think anti-God doesn't exist, I can't find any real villains—only victims.

But when I wonder:

> *If it wouldn't please God and it doesn't benefit mankind, who does stand to profit from such dishonesty?*

Wallace Murphree

the answer that seems obvious is Belief-premium Christianity itself. If I may personify the movement, I see it as having taken on a villainous life of its own, where it thrives and proliferates by the self-reproducing tactics of dishonest belief.

So while I once thought Belief-premium Christianity to be the absolute standard of righteousness and holiness, it now seems to be a travesty of it; and while I once thought it to be God's merciful plan to save the fallen race, it now seems to be a vicious scheme that propagates itself by exploiting the sincerest and best. For it takes otherwise scrupulously honest adults and turns them into deceivers of the youth, and it commandeers the highest love of parents and uses it to brainwash their children. And this dishonesty *naturally* produces conditions that are favorable for its own survival and growth for, like victims of a contagious disease (or a chain letter), those who are infected by it *naturally* convert into transmitters of it. Accordingly—and contrary to what I once held—there seems to be no reason to suppose providential support for Belief-premium Christianity; instead, its inherent mechanism for self-propagation explains how it thrives as a matter of *natural selection* through the generations of its human hosts.

But ironically, this quasi-Darwinian account seems to exemplify one of the basic Christian tenets I was taught as a child, viz., that nature, itself, is depraved.

Love-premium Christianity

But not all Christians are Belief-premium Christians—: the Apostles' Creed contains no article to the effect that we ought to believe or that God wills that we believe. Accordingly, there are those who—although actual believers themselves—do not hold that they are fulfilling a duty by believing, or that it is the key to salvation. Rather, they hold that God knows how to judge right and mercifully concerning issues of salvation, and they are quite willing to leave it for him to do. In fact, their faith *is* their trust in God concerning such

From Faith to Doubt...and Life as a Failed Believer

matters; and this faith frees them from fear of being penalized for holding an incorrect view. That is, it releases them from worry about eternal destination, and frees them to live a life of Christian love in the here and now.

Indeed, these Christians might see any religious preoccupation with the maintenance and propagation of the correct belief system as itself a display of faithlessness—as a failure to trust God, and as an attempt to save themselves and their loved ones by a type of intellectual good work. Also, they might even endorse Tennyson's famous line that "There lives more faith in honest doubt...than in half the creeds."

My childhood religion taught that these are not "real Christians," and presented Biblical passages to show how such imposters stood to incur special disfavor on Judgment Day. But, of course, these "imposters" have different interpretations of the passages and, perhaps, a different view of the status of the Bible as well. And they see "belief-evangelism" as a perversion of Christianity, and the so-called "Great Commission" as a distortion of a private conversation Jesus reportedly had with his disciples.

Although outsiders typically downplay the matter as a mere in-family squabble between the more conservative and the more liberal wings of Christianity, it seems to me that their difference is categorical, rather than merely a matter of degree. So, although both populations are Christian in that both accept the Apostles' Creed and both strive to do what they believe Christ commanded, they have the feel of completely different religions to me; and my diatribe is only against the one, and not the other.

I think there must be many who are torn between these conflicting views, especially when they have to decide between what seems to be the caring thing at the moment and what would be more likely to win the soul to Christianity in the long run. In my own Christian life I told myself there was no conflict, but I never quite felt confident about it and I think I must have wavered quite a bit. Moreover, I think that

Wallace Murphree

wavering may be a frequent occurrence for many conscientious Christians as they try to obey The Golden Rule and The Great Commission at the same time.

My missionary sister, Sarah, tells the story of such an incident. Once she and Ken, along with a few laypersons, had a meeting scheduled with two Arabic men to discuss religion. One of the laywomen had spent great periods of time praying and preparing her testimony in hopes that God could use it to help lead these men to Christ. When the time came, one of the Arabic men began by summarizing Islam. When asked why he believed it, he surprised the Christians by saying he hadn't believed it for many years—that he had become a scientist and an atheist, and that the religion is a superstition. As his story then unfolded, it turned out that his devout Moslem parents had worked hard to get tuition for the very education that led him to reject Islam, and that they now were tormented with the guilt that they put his soul on the path to hell. He said he had tried to reason with them but, since he "could not reason with their superstition," he remains an atheist and the family remains broken.

Now this was not the discussion the Christians had prepared for at all, and they lost track of time and the two men had to leave before the missionaries had a chance to say much. But as they departed, the laywoman who had prepared her testimony so diligently demanded a quick audience; then, as forcefully as she knew how, she reprimanded the young scientist for betraying the trust of his parents, and exhorted him to return and do whatever it took to become reunited with them.

Sometime after the meeting was over she was suddenly horrified, for only then did she realize what she had done—: she had let her emotions get the best of her and had literally forgotten all about the testimony she had prepared. Worse yet, she even so much as endorsed his return to the non-Christian religion of his childhood!

Later the scientist was reported to have said that Christian evangelism is simply an effort to propagate a belief system. "Although they all

From Faith to Doubt...and Life as a Failed Believer

claim it's the religion of love," he said, "no Christian missionary or evangelist has ever challenged me to lead a life of love. Instead, every one I've ever heard has simply tried to convince me to accept their beliefs. Well..., at least almost every one," he corrected himself; "once there was this lay missionary lady who just scolded me for deserting my parents, and implored me to re-establish the relationship with them that I had all but given up on.

Chapter 7 Hurting Those Who Cared

I think the onset of my questioning came as a surprise to Martha; however, at first I think she assumed it would be a temporary affair, as did I. But as it was prolonged, especially during one period of graduate school, it became a problem for us or, I should say, my handling it became a problem.

During this period I would often come home from classes excited about new skeptical insights I had had. She would always listen politely and then go about her chores. It bothered me that she seemed unaffected by the points I thought so important. I wanted her to agree; or, if not, I wanted her to argue—to give me the chance to show her where she was wrong. I'm sure what I really wanted was for her to be just as skeptical as I, but she was not to be moved. And the longer she remained steadfast the more insistently I badgered, until someone finally made me aware of what an awful thing it was that I was doing.

So far as I know, once I quit trying to convince her of skepticism, our differences in this respect have not been a major source of distress for her. Of course, she has missed out on having the Christian family she had always envisioned and the church life we had planned together. But she has never accused me of having betrayed her in the matter, and I believe she has not felt spiritual anguish over my "lost soul."

As I look back on it now I think the questions I wanted Martha to appreciate concerned the evil I saw in Belief-premium Christianity, while the religion she saw no reason to question was that of the love-premium variety. So, I think my perception of whatever differences we had was blown out of proportion by my failure to realize this distinction then.

From Faith to Doubt...and Life as a Failed Believer

I never went to church in Nashville but Martha continued to attend when we moved there. Then she became active in church when we moved Starkville and I frequently watched the Sunday morning worship service on local television. Then when they got old enough to have a preference, Scott and Kate were allowed to decide for themselves whether to attend; however, "for the sake of appearances" all of us would go to church on the Sundays we were visiting our parents in Alabama. Usually we all went to Martha's home church instead of my home church in Wedowee.

I was honest with my parents about my skepticism. In turn, they responded to my confession of doubt respectfully; for example, they never called on me to "say grace" over a meal, or to lead the prayer at family devotions after I told them I could no longer do so in earnest. Of course, they hoped, and I think believed, that this would be a temporary state for me. In fact, it seemed difficult for them to understand how any person could fail to see that there must be a God, and they struggled to understand how I could be in doubt about it.

I mentioned earlier than Dad thought it could be the result of my smoking, and that I would be able to see the truth if I quit. However, later I learned from my siblings that he had also explored the possibility that maybe I was saved after all, but that I was just reluctant to use the names of *Jesus* and *God* in connection with it. They reported that he would remark of my better behavior from time to time, "I just believe that I see the spirit of Jesus showing in those actions," or, "I just don't believe he would have behaved that way if he were really a sinner." Etc. Perhaps one reason he never could rest in that idea was that I continued to smoke.

I was aware of the anguish I was causing my parents all along. They literally believed this world is a testing ground on one's way to eternal beatitude or eternal woe, and I think their greatest fear was that one (or some) of their children would be lost. However, when we were together they never belittled my doubts or tried to pressure or argue me into believing, although occasionally Daddy would give me a book as we left. But we always enjoyed our time together very much when we visited; and when it came time for devotions they would always sing a few extra hymns because they knew I liked them so much.

For years one of Daddy's favorites was "Be Still, My Soul"; I remember once after we had sung it, maybe a year or two before he died, he remarked that the last couplet of the last verse (in our hymnbook) was among his best-loved lines ever:

> Be Still My Soul: when change and tears are past,
> All safe and blessed we shall meet at last.[11]

After our initial discussions about my skepticism, he and I then avoided extended talks about my personal beliefs for decades, although I knew it weighed heavily on him all along. Finally—not long before he died—he wrote to ask me where I stood on the issues after all this time.

I wrote a long letter back, in which I tried to justify my skepticism in his eyes. I remember spending several pages on the Problem of Evil, and I also told him that as I saw it, he "gave his life to Christ" as a very young lad, and then he spent his whole adult life honoring that childhood promise. And, I proposed that while this said something magnificent about his character, the result was that his whole adult worldview was based on, and no more conceptually justified than, the beliefs of that little boy.

---

[11] Katharina Von Schlegel (Tr. By Jane L. Borthwick)

From Faith to Doubt...and Life as a Failed Believer

I have often regretted writing that for it must have hurt to read that one of his sons thought his whole life's work was so specious. On the other hand, I have always been glad I edited out the account of my struggle with the Eskimo boy's religion—that then I relied on his fatherly protection from false doctrine but I now realize it was in the credulity of his boyhood that I had unwittingly placed my trust.

I certainly had not wanted to be insensitive or unkind by either of the two boyhood remarks; but I felt I should lay my perception of things out as frankly as possible because I assumed this correspondence was the beginning of what would become an extended exchange.

He complimented the "logic" of my presentation of the Problem of Evil when he responded, and agreed that it would be wrong to serve a master who would allow any injustice. But, he contended, that from the perspective of everlasting life God would surely allow no unjustified suffering. In fact, Daddy was a very sensitive to the suffering around him, and liberally dedicated his efforts and resources toward the alleviation of misery. Apart from the doctrine of The Fall we had never talked about the problem of evil, but I knew he believed God would fully compensate for any undeserved earthly affliction in the final resolution of things.

Concerning my claim that his whole religious life had no more justification than his boyhood experience, he remonstrated that God had continually reaffirmed that youthful insight, so the truth revealed to him then had become increasingly clearer, and his understanding of it had grown progressively deeper with each passing day. However, he suggested that we might discuss that more if we had time later but that at the present he was especially interested in one question: Was I ready to die? He said he had no doubt about any of my siblings, but that, despite his continued prayers, he could not help but still worry about me. Of course, I was not surprised.

It was hard for me to reply to his direct question as to whether I was ready to die. I drafted two or three responses, but was in no hurry because I assumed I had plenty of time. However, before I got the letter completed he had a stroke, and died a week later.

It didn't occur to me then that he may have had a premonition about his impending death and that his decision to open this topic again was a final and desperate attempt to help a lost son find the way. However, Tal later told me he thought he had had some "warning"—perhaps a mini-stroke or two.

Daddy couldn't speak after he had the stroke, and I think he must have lost all language capacity because he couldn't signal answers to questions even though he had complete use of one hand and arm. However, otherwise it seemed that he was fully aware and alert.

I drove to Wedowee soon after he was admitted to the hospital and pretty much just watched as the caregivers tended to him. But I returned later in the week and was able to spend some time with Mother and him, and then with him alone. When I got there, Mother led me in to see him. I took his good hand and apologized for not having answered his letter yet, "...so now I'll tell you face to face: Yes, I am ready to die." Mother's reaction seemed to show she was aware of what he had written, because she immediately exclaimed, "Hobart, did you hear him? Wallace said he IS ready to die! Did you hear him?"

After a while Mother left us to be alone, and we looked into each other's eyes and wept. A line from an old Civil War poem he used to recite came to mind: "...the heart must speak when the lips are

From Faith to Doubt...and Life as a Failed Believer

dumb."[12] So, I tried to tell him with my heart how much I loved him, and how sorry I was for the suffering I had caused. I thought he understood in a way—that is, I felt he was aware of the "tone of my emotions." Of course, I wondered if he had really understood what I had claimed and, if so, if he knew or suspected that it was only half-true (for I could only use "ready to die" in one sense while I knew he used it in another). I wondered if he smelled cigarette smoke on me.

I had been leaning over his raised bed during this time. When I thought it appropriate to release our clasped hands I started to straighten up, but he held me firm—and we talked with our heart for much longer. I wanted to sing "Be Still My Soul," but I was sure I had no more control over my voice than he had over his; so I sang it with my heart to him as my tears continued to flow.

I became aware of footsteps that stopped outside the door. It was the doctor—a long-time family friend—who had paused to give us another minute. Then he entered, and I bade Daddy goodbye.

Driving back to Starkville I kept thinking of the anguish he had suffered on my account—*and I hated the religion that would not allow me to doubt without making him suffer for it.*

The next word I got was from Sarah—: "Wallace, Daddy has 'gone home'."

He turned 86 in the hospital a day or two before he died. Mother was 12 years younger, and we siblings and our families continued to get

---

[12]Kate Putman Osgood, "Driving Home the Cows," in *An American Anthology, 1787-1900,* ed. Edmund Clarence Stedman (Boston: Houghton Mifflin, 1900), 868.

together with her whenever we could. I am convinced that Mother understood the limitation of my "testimony" to Daddy on his deathbed because she never called on me to pray during family devotions on these visits; so the problem of how to keep from hurting my father began to replay itself for Mother. Of course, I am sure she felt the fear for my future as intensely as he all along, but she had always had him to lean on and to be their spokesperson before.

When I retired Martha and I moved back to the family property to build the log cabin we had always dreamed of, but I was very uneasy for fear my presence would exacerbate this problem for Mother. She still attended the church we children grew up in, although she was in her nineties and signs of dementia were beginning to show. After we got settled in a bit, Martha and I went to church one Sunday, and then also the next. We were warmly received by old friends and the new membership as well. Later in the afternoon of that second Sunday Mother called over and chatted some, and after a bit she got confused and thought she was talking to Tal. She said, "Wallace and Martha came to church again today. Of course, sinners will come to church for a few Sundays from time to time, but they always drop out. But if Wallace and Martha continue to come, I can rest easy and know that he is really saved." (Incidentally, neither she nor Daddy ever had any doubts about Martha.)

As I suppose most anyone would have done under the circumstances, I took advantage of that exceptionally bad piece of theology and began attending regularly.

Mother's eyesight worsened steadily, and her dementia progressed until she became unable to endure a church service; but she continued to live with Sarah and Ken for well over a year before we finally felt we should put her in a nursing home. When I visited her during these months I would always wheel her chair to the piano and play the old hymns and, in her broken voice, she would join me and sing verse after verse of each from memory. But she and I never discussed the question of my faith after Daddy died.

From Faith to Doubt...and Life as a Failed Believer

***

Martha and I have continued our church participation. In fact, I look forward to the sermons each week and enjoy the music very much; and, while I do not take the Holy Communion or affirm The Apostles' Creed, no one seems to consider my incomplete participation a matter of disrespect—if they notice it at all. Moreover, both Martha and I support its several outreach programs, and take pleasure its friendship gatherings and social events. Indeed, we both feel very fortunate for this body of companionship we have come to feel a part of. And it's pretty awesome for me to be back in the same sanctuary where so much of my childhood and youth was spent, and where each pew holds some special memory. And, for what it's worth, it is a joy to feel a part of a church community with Martha again—for the first time since the very early years of our marriage.

Chapter 8 Living in Doubt

I think it is not easy for a person steeped in one view to understand what holding an opposing view must be like. Rather, different outlooks typically seem so outrageous that they are easily caricatured as being simplistic if not downright evil and such, I think, is often the case when the lifelong Christian considers what the outlook of a nonbeliever must be like—and vice versa.

Furthermore, I think it may be easy for Christians to make the supposition that all nonbelievers in God must feel pretty the same way when it comes to what they do believe. However, this is not the case at all. Rather, in the same way that "nonrepublicans" include not only democrats, but also libertarians, communists, neo-Nazis, anarchists, etc., "nonbelievers" likewise include thinkers from every cranny of the nontheistic spectrum. And, for what it's worth, in the same way that being a democrat is much "closer" to being a republican than it is to being a neo-Nazi (although both democrats and neo-Nazis are "nonrepublicans"), I consider my overall outlook much closer to Love-premium Christianity than it is to many other positions of nonbelief.

I shall attempt to describe what my own outlook as a nonbeliever is by responding to four questions that Christians often ask. They are:

If you don't believe in God, then…

1. do you say that physical matter is all that exists?
2. how can you still believe in right and wrong?
3. what *do* you put your faith in?
4. what will you do in the face of death?

From Faith to Doubt...and Life as a Failed Believer

These are questions I thought very important when I was a Christian, and they are ones that have subsequently been posed to me most often by Christians. Moreover, they mark concerns that Christian students typically raised against agnosticism and atheism in my classes.

Reality

The question is: *If one doesn't believe in God then doesn't he or she believe that physical matter is all that exists?*

The short answer is "not necessarily;" but I shall elaborate some and summarize my own view.

Ontology is that sub-branch of philosophy concerned with the general question as to what kinds of things exist, and I think this branch of inquiry is most easily approached by considering the traditional mind-body problem. (I mentioned earlier that my dissertation was on the mind-body problem.)

In general, *the mind-body problem* refers to the set of difficulties faced when trying to account for both the subjective and the objective features of the world in one coherent world-picture. That is, on the one hand we believe that there are subjective things such as pains, hopes, wishes, thoughts, dreams, etc., and on the other we believe there are objective things such things as electrons, atoms, molecules, rocks, planets, etc. So, the problem is to make sense out of how these two widely different kinds of things can hang together to constitute one world and, especially, how both can be ingredient in a human being.

One view, *ontological materialism,* contends that physical matter is what is "really real" for it is what molecules, rocks, etc. are actually made of. Of course, proponents of this view do not say that wishes, thoughts, etc. are also *made of* matter, but they hold that these are states or processes of one's brain which is made of matter, and so they are reducible to matter. Of course, today matter is conceived in terms of physical energy (rather than "material stuff"), but the words, *matter, materialism,* etc., linger as conveniences.

Although this view has always been popular among atheists, it is not entailed by atheism.

A prevalent alternative view in Western philosophy has been *ontological idealism* (from "idea," as "idea[l]ism"), which contends that minds are the "really real" things, and that atoms, molecules, rocks, and planets are, so to speak, nothing but *ideas* in human minds and/or in the infinite mind of God. There are various versions of this general theme, but they hold in common that physical matter does not exist as an objective, independent substance.

Although ontological idealism tends to gain adherents as it is studied, students usually report that it seems far-fetched and even absurd upon first consideration.

In fact, both of these "monistic" theories seem unsatisfactory to many people. Accordingly, common sense seems to have accepted the combined view (*ontological dualism*) which holds that minds and matter are both independently real.

According this view, objective things—electrons, rocks, etc.—are made of matter, while subjective things—hopes, thoughts, etc.—are properties of minds. (In this context the terms *mind, soul,* and *spirit* are used interchangeably, as all refer to an *im*material substance.)

Moreover, this view holds that the mind inhabits and animates the material body while it is alive, and that there is interaction between the two. In general, the mind *directs* the body by its decisions, while the body *informs* the mind by means of perception; that is, the body literally serves as the "eyes and ears" for the mind. But it is not as if a person *has* a mind; rather, on this view the person *is* the mind (soul, or spirit) and it *has* a body which it animates.

From Faith to Doubt...and Life as a Failed Believer

Death, then, is the mind's leaving the body, at which time the mind becomes a disembodied spirit and the body becomes a mere corpse. So if one accepts this dualistic view it seems easy—even philosophically necessary—to accept a belief in afterlife; and if one accepts the afterlife of disembodied human spirits it seems easy enough to accept the possibility of other spirits, like angels and the infinite spirit of God. In fact, I think most Christians I knew growing up would pay lip service to Creedal belief in the resurrection of the body (a religious miracle), but then would otherwise talk of afterlife in terms of disembodied souls (a philosophically necessity). That is, they contended that upon disembodiment the soul would go to heaven or hell, and the body would return to dust.

But the general position of ontological dualism supports the possibility that the spirits should linger on earth in a disembodied state, or become reincarnated in other human or animal bodies. Furthermore, while the general view is compatible with the belief in the existence of God, it does not entail it. That is, one could believe that there is no God, but that human subjectivity is not reducible to physical matter.

Each of these three views has had its share of criticisms. For example, critics of the two monistic views contend the neither is sufficient to account for everything that exists, and that both finally have to explain by "explaining away." On the other hand, critics of dualism contend that it depicts the two kinds of reality (mind and matter) as being so radically different from each other that it is difficult to see how they can combine to form one unified world. For example, it is difficult to conceive of a human organism as "a soul plus its corpse," and to understand how the soul can move the physical corpus around simply by making decisions.

However, each of these views has had brilliant defenders, and each continues to have its share of adherents today. Indeed, with the advent of robots and advancements in genetics and neurophysiology, there has been a revival of materialism in the past half-century. However, many people, including myself, have found each of these general positions unsatisfactory and have looked for other alternatives.

The view that seems most satisfactory to me is the one advanced in the "process philosophy" of Alfred North Whitehead. [1861-1947] In fact, my dissertation consisted of a defense of this view over the then-latest version of materialism.

What Whitehead proposes is that the very basic units of reality all have both an "interiority" and an "exteriority," and that these two "dimensions," like the inside and the outside of a circle, are inseparable. Then, for Whitehead, it is in terms of these inseparable, but distinguishable, dimensions that the respective subjective and objective features of reality are to be accounted for. That is, science, by its very nature, inspects the exterior aspects of things, and describes these in the objective language of physics, chemistry, biology, etc. The interiority of things, however, is private and scientifically "un-get-at-able"; however, it is the dimension where the scientist's thoughts, beliefs, etc., occur.

So, from the perspective of objective science, physicists speak of quanta of energy; but a quantum of energy is not objective through and through; rather, it is a "droplet of experience." That is, even in its most simple form, a quantum of energy is a pulsation—a "throb." So the full picture is that the basic units of reality are of quanta of *"experiential energy"*; that is, both subjective and objective elements go into the constitution of everything.

But Whitehead is certainly not saying that everything is conscious. Rather, on his view the subjective dimension is very negligible, dim, and completely unaware in the makeup of inorganic elements; however, rudimentary forms of life occur wherever the subjective dimension is more pronounced, and the so-called higher forms of life, including human beings, emerge as this dimension becomes progressively more important. But even for the most highly

From Faith to Doubt…and Life as a Failed Believer

sophisticated pulsations in the human brain, "consciousness flickers," and its intensity is always a matter of degree.

One important implication of this view is that since there cannot be an interior without an exterior, there cannot be a disembodied subjectivity, or mind. So, any afterlife would require an exteriority of some kind; but Whitehead finds no reason to postulate an afterlife at all.

However, Whitehead's system does include a God of sorts, and an associated theory he calls *"objective* immortality." The theory is that when an experience—i.e. a "throb"— is over and past it doesn't just fall into nonexistence, but that it is preserved in the being of God instead. So, each past event of the entire world—including every living person's past—is there in God's eternal repository today. And when one's life is over it, along with everything it was contemporary with, will be eternally preserved. Furthermore, these preserved events are not just archived and forgotten but, rather, each is eternally judged by God, and then perpetually re-judged in light of the never-ending inclusion of new events, as each present moment lapses into the past. So, while *living one's life* is a temporal process, *the life lived*—i.e., the product produced by this process—is eternally preserved in God. In fact, it is this past, temporal world (which includes our pasts) that constitutes the objective dimension of God—: it is the "body of God," so to speak.

Of course, this is not the God of my childhood, and I suppose most would not see it as the God of Christianity. However, its study is included in the offerings of quite a few Christian divinity schools under the name of *Process Theology.*

Still, like the God of my childhood, I am skeptical as to whether Whitehead's God exists. Incidentally, the advisor of my dissertation, a preeminent Whitehead scholar, argued that Whitehead's general system of thought—his world-picture—is theoretically stronger when the notion of God is expunged from it.[13]

But, in either case, the view is far removed from ontological materialism which Christians often suppose is the only alternative to theism.

Ethics

The question is: *If one doesn't believe in God, how can he or she still believe in right and wrong?*

My general conception as to what ethics is all about has changed since my preministerial student days, and I also feel no obligation to many of the specific taboos and duties of my childhood any longer. Still I believe that some things are right and other things are wrong as strongly, if not more strongly, than ever.

However, as a Christian I didn't understand how there could be any right and wrong without God, because I understood right and wrong simply to be obedience or disobedience to God's commandments. So on that view, if there were no God, there would be no divine commandments and, therefore, there would be no duty and everything would be morally permissible.

---

[13] Donald W. Sherburne, "Whitehead Without God," *The Christian Scholar*, L, 3 (Fall 1967).

From Faith to Doubt…and Life as a Failed Believer

However, I have come to believe that ethical principles stand on their own—much like the laws of math or logic—and that, accordingly, they hold whether there is a God who has spelled them out as commandments or not.

In fact, it now seems to me that the mere obedience to a creator's commandments cannot be what makes an action right because if the creator had been anti-God he would have commanded us to do evil. So, a creator would have to issue an ethically valid commandment in order for it to be our duty to obey it; and even then it would not be obedience to the commander that would make it right but, rather, the validity of the principle that was commanded.

Incidentally, this apparently was Sarah's view all along for, rather than accepting Jesus' ethics because she thought he was divine, she accepted his divinity because she thought the ethics he taught was correct.

But even granting there would still be right and wrong without God, the believer might ask what motive a nonbeliever could have for doing right instead of wrong if there is no God to administer reward and punishment in an afterlife.

I was impressed by this consideration as a teenager; in fact, I remember trying to visualize what I would do with my life if I ever came to believe there was no God. One scenario I tried to follow through would start with my robbing a bank; then I would fill my life with as much pleasure as money could buy until I got caught, and then I would commit suicide before I could be punished. But realistically I felt sure I'd be too big a coward for that, although I seriously thought I would do something essentially like that, but just less drastic. That is, I thought I would attempt to maximize my own earthly pleasure. It simply seemed there would be no reason not to, if doing right or wrong carried no reward or punishment in an afterlife.

Wallace Murphree

Now, however, I doubt very seriously that there is an afterlife, and—so far as I know myself—I have no fear that I might go to hell. And, while I've never been seriously tempted to rob a bank, I must admit that my anticipation of a punishment-free "after-death" has probably had a significant influence my subsequent behavior. However, I don't see that it has made me "less ethical" at all—at least if "being ethical" is understood to mean "doing right for right's sake" as my religion actually taught.

On the contrary, on the very view my religion taught, my abstaining from worldly pleasure *for fear it would send me to hell* was never ethical to begin with. Of course it was prudent (given my beliefs) but, rather than being right for right's sake, it was just "looking out for old number one." In fact, as I look back I think the threat of hell overwhelmed most any chance I had to do right for right's sake when I was a believer; so, in an important way, I think my skepticism has provided an opportunity to be ethical that I didn't have before.

But the more significant problem I have with ethics as a skeptic occurs when I consider that doing right today may be of no importance in an everlasting future without God or eternal life.

For example, it doesn't upset me much today to think that one caveman murdered another thousands of years ago. Of course, I know it was brutal and tragic at the time, but now that it's over and there's no one left who cares, its horror and tragedy seem to have "expired" and now it is simply a dry historical fact. So if I were granted the power to change the past and undo that murder, I'm not sure I would feel a strong need to do it because it simply seems not to matter very much, if at all, anymore.

Furthermore, after the sun has burned out and the human race has perished and there is no one left to think about it ever again, it seems by then the murder clearly would not matter at all. And, to generalize, perhaps once there is no one left to care about anything, it will never matter what went on any time before.

From Faith to Doubt...and Life as a Failed Believer

To me it is a very sobering thought that nothing should amount to anything in the final analysis. That is, although human love, kindness, and courage were wonderful while they lasted, it seems tragic that they should be forever lost and forgotten. And while deceptions, betrayals, and cruelty were horrendous while they were going on, it seems sad that the perpetrators should finally get off free, and that there should be no lasting memorial to the victims.

But if there is no God or afterlife there will be no lasting recognition of any event that went on before, and so it then will not matter what happened. And if for all eternity it will not matter what happened today, it seem groundless to claim that anything now *really* matters today.

Although its hell-punishment always seemed unjustly severe to me, a very great attraction of the religion of my childhood was that it taught that things do matter in the long run—and so there was reason to believe that what we do really matters each day. Furthermore, a beauty of Whitehead's view is that God preserves the value of the present even without an afterlife of rewards and punishments for his creatures. That is, he preserves the value, for he never tires of re-treasuring the noble efforts of our past; and our ignoble deeds suffer perpetual infamy in his everlasting judgment.

But, if there is no eternal evaluator, it seems that value cannot last; and, again, a value that does not last seems hardly a value at all. Accordingly, it seems the belief that there is no God might reasonably lead one to a sort of cosmic nihilism.

Furthermore, I confess I have actually experienced flashes of this nihilistic outlook, especially in moments of despair or in the throes of failure. Moreover, I certainly do not know that it is not correct, and that we deceive ourselves by thinking that something actually matters. However, with the exception of these flashes, I still believe—I don't know how not to believe—that things do matter today whether they matter in the long run or not.

For example, my own selfish desires matter to me today; and even when I tell myself they don't matter in the long run, I still care about them at the moment. In addition, my concerns for my loved ones and friends do not feel any less intense when I think they may not matter in the long run, and the same is the case when I widen my outlook to ethical concerns in general. That is, I feel I ought to do the right today whether it has any long-range status or not; indeed, I feel I ought to do it for its own sake here and now, and the realization that it may not finally count for anything does not lessen the obligatory character of that feeling.

Furthermore, although I am no longer impressed by many of my specific childhood taboos, *what* I now believe to be right and wrong is essentially what I think that Jesus taught when it is extracted from its supernatural context.

For example, when I was in grammar school a missionary speaking in our church said his organization could get New Testaments to mission fields in Africa for a nickel each; furthermore, he said that on an average one heathen was converted to Christianity with each New Testament they sent out. Of course to me that meant that a soul could be saved from hell for a nickel. I didn't get much money back then (maybe a nickel every week or two) but it seemed clear at once what I ought to do with the nickels I did get—: although I wanted to buy a Nehi strawberry drink (reluctantly permitted by my father) with each at recess, I *knew* I should use it to "buy" some soul's freedom from hell instead. And as I look back, I do not find fault with my childhood ethics in the matter at all. Indeed, when the supernatural claims are removed, it is by that very same ethic that today I feel it is immoral to enjoy the luxury of a Western lifestyle when children in other lands are literally dying for lack of goods this money could have supplied.

I fully accept Jesus' teaching that we should feed the hungry, visit the sick, clothe the naked, etc. Indeed, I wonder if I don't believe this more strongly than many Christians do. In fact, I know I feel it more strongly than I did when I was a Christian, because as a Christian I

From Faith to Doubt...and Life as a Failed Believer

took the misery of earthly starvation, loneliness, and exposure to be insignificant when compared to eternity.

When Karl Marx said religion is the opiate of the people, he meant that it deadens the daily hunger of the masses by promising them abundance in the hereafter. However, I wonder if it is not also the opiate that deadens the conscience of affluent Christians as they, after giving a pittance, allow the masses to go hungry while they enjoy the excesses their wealth affords. At any rate, for nonbelievers generally there is no by-and-by when the earthly malnutrition and starvation can ever be made right. Rather, the only time this evil can be defeated is the present. Likewise, for them if there is ever to be justice, if wrongs are ever to be made right, if the abandoned are ever to be loved, and if there is ever to be kindness, forgiveness, or reconciliation it must be today. This, to me, is the true message of "secular humanism," which has been so vilified by so many Christians.

Certainly the outlook of erstwhile Christians change drastically when they lose the faith. Perhaps some of them do become bank robbers and many, no doubt, turn to a life in search of personal pleasure. However, there are many others who, upon losing the faith, merely shift their effort from trying to save souls from hell to trying to save kids from drugs, disease, poverty, etc.

So, along with this latter group, I accept that there is intrinsic, or self-justifying, value in the temporal world, and that its inherent worthiness does not depend on whether it is to be finally preserved or lost. And this not only prevents ethics from being meaningless but also lends a special urgency and seriousness to it. That is, the urgency of leading lost souls to Christ is now replaced by the urgency stemming from the awareness that epidemics are spreading and people are starving and others are being raped, maimed, tortured, and slaughtered—*right now at this very minute*. Of course, this is not to claim that I always, or even often—or even ever—do what I believe I ought with regard to such matters. In fact, my lifestyle has hardly ever been approved by my conscience. But now the guilt I feel lies in having let my fellow human being down, rather than in having disobeyed a supernatural authority.

Faith

The question is: *If one doesn't believe in God, then what do they put their faith in?*

No doubt religion has been the source of numerous important insights, and I think the greatest of these may be the realization that we do not have it within our power to save ourselves. The fact is that we did not create ourselves, nor could we help having been created. And we do not have the ability to provide an afterlife for ourselves if that is not the way of things, and we do not have the ability to refuse an afterlife if it is the way of things. And as we bide our time on earth we are not in command of very much, even of our own bodies. For example, compared to many other animals, even the most dexterous of us is relatively clumsy; and the temporary paralysis of a limb (as comes "from having slept the wrong way") shows even our most rudimentary abilities to be dependent on involuntary workings completely beyond our control.

So in addition to being *ir*religious, any belief of self-sufficiency is folly as well. Accordingly, when we realistically admit the precariousness of our situation, it seems we have to entrust our ultimate concerns to something or someone outside ourselves, for we would otherwise be overwhelmed by our insecurity.

In response, the person who honestly believes that God exists can say: "All right, God, I place all worries and cares about the things over which I have no control into your hands, and I turn loose of them myself." Then I submit that the freedom that results to be a rational and even a *virtuous* state. Indeed, I wonder if the ethics Jesus taught doesn't require this type of freedom, for it seems difficult to be

From Faith to Doubt…and Life as a Failed Believer

authentically involved in loving one's neighbor or caring for the sick when one's mind is preoccupied with one's own worries.

Indeed, if such freedom *is* the Christian "virtue of faith" then perhaps the "sin of unbelief" is not that of atheism or agnosticism at all; rather, it could be sin theists commit when they fail to entrust their welfare to God that they believe to exist, and continue to try to save themselves instead—by doing the right deeds, or by holding the right beliefs.[14]

From this view of the nature of faith there clearly appears a fundamental deficiency in the nonbeliever's worldview, since it has no God to serve as the trustee. So, what can nonbelievers trust? What *can* they put their faith in?

In my early doubting I worried that I might be making the most dreadful of all mistakes—a mistake that would send me to hell, and prevent me from providing a warning to others; and, of course, the more I doubted God's existence, the more my outlook lacked the very trustee on whom a Christian would be able to cast his or her deepest cares.

However, I eventually came to be at peace with my doubts by simply leaving such matters to the "nature of being"—for lack of a better phrase for it. That is, I determined (as nearly as I can word it) that: "Worrying does not help, and I can't do anything that does. So, I let go of it, and accept whatever is decreed by the structure of reality."

---

[14]Cf. Robert M. Adams, "The Virtue of Faith," *Faith and Philosophy,* Vol. 1, No. 1 (January 1984): 10.

Of course, it doesn't make much sense to say "I accept" when there is no possible way to resist. However, I found that the determination "to let the chips fall where they may in an accepting spirit" granted me the freedom to question, and the freedom to doubt whatever then seemed questionable. And I submit that this move is available to atheists and agnostics generally. That is, I propose that in want of a personal God to cast their ultimate cares on, the atheist and agnostic can consign these matters to the nature of being itself, and leave them there.[15]

After I came to be at peace with my doubts I realized *my freedom to question was nothing other than my release from the compulsion to try to save myself.* Also, a little later it dawned on me that turning loose of religious concerns by leaving them to the nature of being was tantamount to the faith that pantheists (who believe that God *is* the world) have always advocated. In fact, if taken to its full extent, I think this notion of faith might include the Christian concept described above, since for the Christian the "nature of being" would be the nature of God and his creation.

Of course, I do not know what the nature of being is like. For all I know, reality may be composed of God and his creation, or anti-God and his; or perhaps there is no supernatural realm at all. So, the faith I propose is not to be reserved for a being whose nature is antecedently known to be good; rather it is in the nature of being—*whatever it is.* Such a faith may seem risky, or even reckless, since one thereby might unwittingly be placing trust in a devil, or in an evil scheme. But

---

[15] See my "Faith for Atheists and Agnostics," *Sophia,* Vol 30, Nos. 2&3 (1991): 59-70. (Reprinted in *Addresses of the Mississippi Philosophical Association*, ed. Bennie R. Crockett, Jr., (Atlanta: Rodopi, 2000), 178-190.

From Faith to Doubt…and Life as a Failed Believer

it may be worth noting that if the God of Christianity is the creator, it is in him, although unnamed, that such faith is ultimately cast.

Of course, Belief-premium Christians are not happy with such a risky concept, for they want a faith that gives assurance. But I think *it is knowledge that gives assurance (and strong belief that gives the feeling of assurance); but what faith gives is freedom.* Accordingly, I propose the Christian faith that casts its cares on its God bestows the freedom necessary for a life of Christian love—as it "saves" the person form life-denying obsessions and worries. But it doesn't guarantee anything, because it leaves it up to God.

Of course, it could be that there is a creator who will save those who believe he exists and send those to torment who honestly do not believe it; but I propose such a creator would be a devil—it would be anti-God, rather than God. And this is not just a sophistical reply for Christian friends; rather, I believe only an evil judge would sentence a person to eternal fire and brimstone for having a mistaken doubt. Of course, there are more "civilized" views of hell. But still, I propose that any eternal punishment for a temporal wrong would infinitely out of proportion, and any moral penalty for an intellectual error would be inherently unjust.

Accordingly, I think my earlier view of Christianity was nearly as if it had a devil on the throne, but I was afraid not to call him "God." At any rate, as I look back I cannot see how my attempt to cling to the faith to keep from offending a possibly existing God was a virtue in any sense. In fact, I think it was cowardly, even though it may have been prudent cowardice. Certainly I was not putting my faith IN him; rather, I was trying to appease him precisely because I didn't trust him otherwise.

Death

The question is: *If one doesn't believe in God, what will he or she do in the face of death?*

Although religion saturates every aspect of the Christian life, it seems especially relevant in the face of death. "It's great to be a Christian when it comes time to die," is a phrase that was often quoted in my childhood, for it was among the last words--and is engraved on the headstone--of my father's preacher brother who died young. Indeed, it is easy to think of religion exclusively in terms of preparation for death and the afterlife that follows. The sinners I knew as a child all planned to get forgiveness before they died, as did I when I made excursions into sin; and there are many deathbed conversions.

At any rate, "death without Christ" always seemed the most hopeless condition imaginable when I was young, for it was the onset of eternal doom. Now, however, I do expect "to die without Christ" and for my earthly life to terminate in the greatest nightmare of my youth for, to my childhood mindset, I expect to be *Lost After All*.

I'm sure I can't predict what feelings I will have if I am alert when the time comes, even though I have tried to think it through several times. I really don't expect to have any new insights, although I surely hope to remain open if any occur. Generally I am skeptical of deathbed intuitions because I suspect the setting tends to be conducive to delusions. However, if in this circumstance I become convinced of what I now doubt, I certainly intend to acknowledge and embrace it. That is, I don't intend *to try* to face death without belief, as if that would be to perform some heroically defiant feat.

Furthermore, if in this circumstance I come to think that belief in God will help my chances *at all* in case there is an afterlife, I suppose I might "grab at this straw." That is, I doubt that I would refuse to profess theism as a matter of ethical principle at that point—although perhaps a skeptic should. However, I feel now, as I described earlier, that if there is a God he would look at least as kindly on honest doubt as he would on the dishonest attempt to adopt this self-serving belief, and I can't imagine what possible insight could make Pascal's wager to the contrary seem cogent again on my deathbed.

From Faith to Doubt...and Life as a Failed Believer

Rather than having a veridical insight, what I think more likely is that I may panic, or that long-repressed horrors from the hell images of my childhood may break through and command my last conscious moments. If this is what happens, I hope any attendants won't think that I'm entering hell, or conclude that hell must exist because I thought I saw it as I was dying.

When I considered myself a sinner, I remember thinking I wouldn't mind dying if I didn't fear hell. However, then when I believed my sins forgiven and felt assured that death would be my entrance into heaven, I still found every realistic thought of my death to be hideous. (I guess I felt sort like a person who idealized marriage, but who was terrified of weddings.) Indeed, it seemed so very horrible that I feared my confidence would falter in the face of it, and I prayed earnestly that when the time came I would be able to die in the faith in which I lived. Also today I don't fear hell but, as before, I still find every realistic thought of my death most revolting. And now, as then, I hope I can die in the faith that I live; i.e., now I hope I can turn loose and let the chips fall where they may.

So although I see no reason to fear my death from ether standpoint, I nevertheless have found the very idea to be shrouded in most horrible fright from both perspectives. I suppose this is natural, and that my case is typical. If so, I think the discrepancy between one's belief and his or her natural emotions sets the stage for possible panic in the actual face of death for anyone; at least, I certainly do no know that I will not panic.

But panic aside, and assuming I don't have other insights between now and then, I feel how I will face death when I think it is at hand should be no different from how I face it now while I still hope it is some distance away.

***

In general, those who believe that persons are eternal souls picture both the *occasion of dying* and the subsequent *state of being dead* one way while those who do not hold the soul substance theory, such as materialists and Whiteheadians, picture it in quite another way.

As was said earlier, the ontological dualists, i.e., those who believe the person is a soul that inhabits a material body in this life, conceive of dying as the person's (final) departure from that body and, as such, it is like leaving a room by "walking through death's door" and into the next phase of existence. Conceived as such a process, each person stands to experience his or her own death, and that experience could well be of joy or distress. For example, the Christianity of my youth taught that the forgiven will be escorted to heaven by a divine presence but that sinners—lost in the darkness—will grope in terror alone. Then, when they reach their respective destinations, the redeemed will live in joy forever and the lost will be eternally damned. So, there could be good reason why the dualist might fear both the occasion of dying and also the subsequent state of being dead.

On the other hand, those who do not believe in the existence of souls ordinarily conceive of personhood in terms of the *experiences* of the human organism, and the person's death then is taken to be the instant immediately following his or her final experience. So, on this view the occasion of dying cannot be experienced because it doesn't occur until the moment immediately following one's final experience. That is, on this view, there is simply "being alive" and then "being dead," and the occasion of death is simply the point where one ends and the other begins.

The ancient Greek materialist, Epicurus [341-270 BCE], advanced this description and it has been widely accepted by those who reject the belief that a person is an enduring soul.

Most who hold this view, including Epicurus, picture such death as something that happens once at the end of each lifetime, and this is

From Faith to Doubt...and Life as a Failed Believer

when the entire life becomes dead, so to speak. However, Whitehead's unusual rendition casts death as *exceedingly* more common than a once-in-a-lifetime affair. In fact, on his view one's ordinary lifetime is composed of a series of "selves-of-the-moment" as one experience, which constitutes one self-of-one-moment, passes away and is followed by another experience, which constitutes the self-of-the-next-moment; etc. Then, according to him, one's lifetime overall is the "perpetual perishing" of the successive selves-of-the-moment, as the experience of the one moment dies away, and the experience of the next comes into being. So, literally, accordingly to Whitehead, each present self dies as it passes, for "to be dead" is simply *is* "to be past." Accordingly, all of one's life up to any given present is already dead in this technical sense; and one will be dead in the practical sense when his or her entire life is in the past. But the passing of one's final self-of-the-moment is only unique in that it has no successor; otherwise, its death—which marks the end of life in the practical sense—is essentially like the death of each of its predecessors.

So according to such thinkers as Epicurus and Whitehead, the occasion of dying holds no real horror for the one facing it, in spite of the fact that people are naturally repulsed by the idea. Furthermore, if there is no continued existence one's own state of being dead cannot be bad for him or her.

Accordingly, if I have no afterlife, then my future state will be no worse for me than my earlier state of having not yet lived—which lasted from the very beginning of time until the "Wallace sperm" won that race back in 1937! Of course, it could be that the state of the world will itself somehow be worse after my death than it was before my birth but, if so, I will no more know or suffer its inferior condition than I knew or enjoyed its superior quality before. In fact, I sort of hate to admit it, but every so often when I think of the possibly bleak future of the planet a voice inside me whispers, "But you've got nothing to worry about, because you'll be dead and gone by then." And sometimes I actually find this to be a comforting thought!

So a scorched earth in its death-throes will mean no more to me then than did the fiery ball of gas composing its original formation. Indeed, the only things bad I can imagine about the state of my being dead concerns others still alive, rather than me. For example, I suppose loved ones will grieve some over my death, my unfinished business will become hardships on others, the evil I have done will continue to have an effect, etc; and if Whitehead's view is correct, God will be forever be disappointed in my shortcomings. But, while such considerations might rightfully concern me now, they will not and cannot bother me then.

So, even though I have what I think is a natural, though irrational, fear of the occasion of dying, I have no such fear of the state of being dead at all—i.e., even for the rest of all time. That is, I don't dread the twenty-second century, or the third millennium, or any time thereafter whatever.

This is how it seems to me that "after-death" will be if there is no afterlife and "this is all there is." I think it is essentially the way that most people conceive the after-death of their pets and animals generally. And although some would see it as degrading the status of humankind, it nevertheless depicts a far kinder and gentler world to me than the one I believed in when I was a Christian. Indeed, I am happy to replace what I believe to be an ego-inflated self-image of humanity with a hell-free future for it.

But this view of a punishment-free future also sacrifices the eternal reward promised to believers, and this is more than many can easily surrender. It would seems especially tragic for those who have spent much their earthly lives in anticipation of a heavenly reunion with departed loved ones for, if this is all there is, they will never see those loved ones again. Indeed, if this is all there is, Daddy's faith and hope that "...all safe and blessed, we shall meet at last," seems but a cruel chimera.

From Faith to Doubt...and Life as a Failed Believer

However, I think this only seems tragic or cruel. What would really be so is if there were an afterlife in which the reunion yearned for did not occur. Then there would be genuine separation. However, if there is no afterlife, we literally will not be separated from each other—just as we were not separated from each other through the ages before we lived—for things must exist to be separate. Likewise, if there is no afterlife, no one will then be disappointed, and Dad will never know nor care that we have not met all safe and blessed.

Being a preacher's kid, I suppose I attended more funerals than most growing up, and I always took great comfort in the promise that there would be a happy reunion. In fact, this picture of a reunion with friends and loved ones has long been a prized religious image for me, and the theme of my best-loved hymns and gospel songs.

And, although I am pleased to believe there will be no afterlife of misery, it truly was, and is, a letdown to accept that there will be no heavenly reunion. But correlative to my doubt of an afterlife is my belief that the passing moments on earth are precious. So rather than trying to picture living blissfully with the saints and angels forevermore, my realistic ideal has become to be sensitive to the suffering in this world and to live in harmony with friends and loved ones in the time that is left. And when a friend dies, I breathe a thanksgiving that the friendship endured to the end—that neither of us yielded to temptations or expediencies that would have ruined it. And, if I am allowed to face my own death in a calm and alert manner, I suppose I would like my last conscious moments to be filled with gratitude for the love and friendship with which I have been so blest; but perhaps it would be more fitting to die in remorse for the suffering that my indulgences failed to prevent.

However, I think what my deathbed sentiments will be is not as important as the sentiments I live by from now until then; for how one faces his or her future will surely make a difference, while whether one approaches life's cessation in gratitude, remorse, or panic will likely be of no further consequence.

Wallace Murphree

***

Such are my responses to the four specific questions about living in doubt. I would also add that, in general, being liberated from the obsession to know the big picture has left me free to live in a world of small beliefs, where I feel very much at home. Of course, the big questions remain, and I still wonder why human beings should ever have existed and why there should have ever been anything at all, etc. And it still seems like something very, very big and important must be going on and I don't what it is. When I conjecture about it I think the answer must lie in some view like Whitehead's philosophy; but, again, I certainly do not know that it does.

But as a skeptic this great unknown is an awe-inspiring mystery, rather than an insecurity; and now I wonder about it as I hope is appropriate for philosophers to wonder, rather than out of the fear that led me into philosophy initially.

Epilogue

As a professor in a state university it was not my prerogative to promote theism, atheism, or skepticism. In fact, this was proscribed by the principle of the separation of church and state. Instead, my charge was to challenge students to study and think hard about these and other philosophical matters for academic reasons.

However, from time to time some student would allege that I was out to tear his or her Christian faith down, although such was never my intention. But I'm sure I actually did spend more time criticizing theism than I did atheism, but this was because my typical class comprised many vocal Christians but only few, if any, atheists. Accordingly, in the ordinary flow of class discussion I was frequently cast in the role of responding to Christian accusations on behalf of the nonbeliever, and I'm sure there were always some who thought I did this too enthusiastically on occasions. I certainly would become frustrated when I felt students perversely refused to understand an opposing position, for one must understand a position in order to appreciate the criticisms of it. For example, if one doesn't understand the Problem of Evil then he or she cannot appreciate any theodicy that is advanced

And also today, while not constrained by the separation of church and state, I still am not an advocate of skepticism, at least not of skepticism *per se*. In fact, skepticism is the name for my failure, for I tried to know—at least, I tried to find what I thought would be good reasons for believing—but I did not succeed.

So, rather than skepticism, what I would recommend is honesty—especially self-honesty, and most especially self-honesty when it conflicts with the call of religious faith. Of course, I believe if self-honesty did prevail then skepticism would flourish as a consequence;

Wallace Murphree

but skepticism, itself, is certainly not the goal, and I only recommend it over dishonest, rather than honest, belief.

***

I don't know what has happened to the student whose paper was mentioned in the Prologue. In fact, I don't remember her name or much about how she looked. I only recall that I found her paper unacceptable because it detailed how her culture had caused her to believe that God exists, while the assignment—given the topic and position on it she chose—asked her to create her own argument for the existence of God. (This was early in the introductory course, before we considered the traditional arguments.) But I don't remember anything else about the case. I suppose I returned the paper and explained the requirement more clearly and that she then submitted another paper that I found to be acceptable.

So, although, the resubmitted work was (presumably) the better one for the class exercise, I think her original paper stood to be the more important one for her personal philosophy—if she took her own report seriously. That is, I think the recognition that one's initial religious beliefs are determined by one's culture is an awesome insight, for it entails that we all would have believed differently except for the accident of our birthplace. Moreover, if our initial belief had been different there is no reason to suppose we would ever have arrived at our present view from that diverse starting point. And, by implication at least, all this was contained in the student's original paper, for she saw and reported that her religious beliefs were culture-bound.

So, short of having a demonstrative proof as to God's existence or an indubitable experience of his presence, I think we must admit that even after our most ardent soul-searching, whether we are theists, atheists, or skeptics today may still be an accident of our birth—: I simply can't say what I would now believe if I had been born an Eskimo.

From Faith to Doubt...and Life as a Failed Believer

Accordingly, I think it behooves us to have intellectual humility when assessing our religious faith and to be modest in the truth-claims we make on the subject; and although I do not advocate skepticism, I strongly recommend listening skeptically to those professing to be in the know. For the cocksure testimony of an affected faith is not only a lie in itself, but it also is a crime against any who might hear and believe it.

LaVergne, TN USA
11 January 2011
211891LV00001B/67/P